MW00571176

# About the Author

Eric Grebler is a technical author, publisher, certified trainer and Linux enthusiast. He has written a variety of computer books on subjects including: operating systems, office suites, graphics publishing and digital audio editing. Having trained thousands of computer users, he knows first hand the trials and tribulations users experience when working with technology.

# Acknowledgments

Putting a book like this together is a huge project and it involves the efforts of many talented individuals. This book wouldn't have happened without the champion efforts of Randy Linnell, who helped facilitate this near impossible task. Thanks are also extended to Mike Garcen and Kevin La Rue who provided me with all the resources needed to get the job done.

Special thanks to Heather MacKenzie for all of her assistance and to Kendall Dawson for lending his technical expertise.

Thanks to my wife Kara and son Ethan for their endless support and inspiration.

# How To Use This Book

Welcome to this No Nonsense Guide™ from Mimosa Books. We hope you enjoy the journey on which your are about to embark, learning about the Linspire operating system. If you are new to this operating system, this book can be used as a self-paced guide or as a reference for whenever you are stuck. If you are upgrading to this latest version, instructions on using the many new and enhanced features are included.

The book presents the material in a visual and procedural format. Rather than burying you in a pile of theoretical information, you are provided with step-by-step instructions that can be used to accomplish many different tasks. Each instruction is accompanied by a screen capture showing you exactly where to click to complete the task. Along the way you will also find dozens of tips and shortcuts for accomplishing your work smarter and faster.

The instructions used in this book are straightforward and no out-of-the-ordinary conventions are used except perhaps one. Occasionally you will see a "|" between certain commands- for example, "Click File | Open." The "|" is a space saver that means "and then click." So the example, "Click File | Open," really means "Click File and then click Open."

As you go through the book you may notice that what you see on your screen may look slightly different than the screen captures you see in the book. Don't worry, this is normal. Depending on how your computer was originally manufactured or configured, there may be slight differences between your computer and the computers that where used for writing this book.

It would take an encyclopedia to cover all of the features that Linspire has to offer, so not every aspect of the operating system is covered here. The goal of this book is to show you how to use those features that are used most often when exploring the world of Linspire.

# Forward

By Michael Robertson, CEO, Linspire Inc.

## Why Linspire?

When I started Linspire, I was accused of being crazy for trying to compete against Microsoft, the world's biggest monolith. But that is precisely the reason why there needs to be competition. Without choice, consumers are treated to a mix of high prices, poor service and a lack of innovation. Choice is good for consumers. Simply put, that is why I started Linspire.

When I started MP3.com, the music industry was very much the same way — it was closed off. The major recording companies controlled music and didn't want to see it on the Internet at all. They sued MP3.com, they sued content providers, they even went after developers of portable MP3 players. But the future cannot be stopped and advancements will happen. Now I can't go to the gym without seeing white headphones leading to MP3 players all around me. Consumers are no longer limited to purchasing expensive CDs. You can buy individual tracks or full albums from sites like MP3tunes.com and within minutes be listening to them on your PC, stereo, or MP3 player.

We are at a time in history where the same thing is happening to the computer operating system. People have endured high prices, viruses, and frequent crashes not because they wanted to, but because there has been a lack of alternatives. In early 2002, I sat around the "lucky table" my father-in-law gave me, feeling that the world was out of balance with one dominating operating system that was leading to expensive pricing, unfriendly licensing and depriving people access to lower-cost computing. So for the last three years, Linspire has been working on creating a viable alternative to restore balance to the world of desktop computing.

# Why Linux?

When I started Linspire, I realized that to compete with Microsoft meant needing to work smarter, not harder. They have more money, more people, and have been producing versions of the Microsoft Windows operating system for more than ten years. That's where Linux came in.

If you're like most people, chances are you only started hearing about Linux recently. While it has been mostly an underground technology used by IT professionals and computer science majors, Linux has been around since the early '90s. Linux itself is based on UNIX, which has been around since 1970. In addition to having years of refinement and experience under its belt, Linux offers some other very big advantages. Unlike Microsoft Windows, which is developed by a specific group of people who all work for a specific company, Linux is developed by a worldwide community.

How does that work? It's through a principle called "open source." Most software companies hide the code that drives their applications, so other people can't take advantage of all the hard work they've put into developing it. Open source is exactly the opposite. Instead of hiding this code, open source does as the name implies and opens the source code to the world, so developers all around the globe can contribute advances and improvements.

By taking advantage of the open source nature of Linux, it's no longer the few people in my three-year-old company competing against Microsoft, it's the thousands of people who have for more than 30 years contributed to making Linux what it is today. This swings the pendulum back in favor of competition. If I were to try competing directly against Microsoft, I would lose. But with the decades of experience and the worldwide community that supports Linux, choice can once again emerge in this long-cornered marketplace.

The one problem with Linux, though, is that it has always been a technical operating system for technical users. Yes, it is very stable and has many advantages over Microsoft Windows, but for most people it has simply been too difficult to be practical. So at Linspire we've been dedicated to crossing the divide and making Linux easy enough for complete novices, while keeping the benefits of security and stability that have made it a favorite among the technical elite.

# Is the Linspire operating system for the masses?

Yes. Linspire is designed with you in mind. We know that most people don't use their PCs for ultra-technical goals like writing computer code or hosting Internet forums. People do write e-mail, surf the web, chat, use an office suite, play games, listen to music, and get pictures from their digital cameras. Linspire comes pre-loaded with all the necessary software to do those things and more.

One of the questions I hear the most is, "Will Linspire run XYZ application that I use?" But after talking to the person who asked it, I find out that the person is never so much tied to that particular application as they are tied to what that application lets them do. It's all about the features and functionality, not about the particular program. The answer I usually give is, "A program made for Microsoft Windows won't run on Linspire, but there are thousands of applications that do run on Linspire and we have one that does just what you want."

Take Microsoft Office for example — that is probably the application that most people want to know about. Why? Because they need a word processor, spreadsheet, and presentation software. They need it to be easy to use, and most importantly they need it to create documents that can be read on a Microsoft Windows computer. Not surprisingly, Microsoft doesn't make their office suite for Linux, but would you really want to waste hundreds of dollars paying for it anyway? Linspire comes with a complete office suite included. That's right...you don't have to spend almost as much on one program as you spent for your computer. The OpenOffice suite included with Linspire has software for word processing, spreadsheets, and presentations, all of which save in the same format as Microsoft Office, so you can read and edit files made by your friends who still use Microsoft Office, and they can read and edit the files you make. If you don't tell anyone, they'll probably never realize that you saved yourself a few hundred dollars and aren't using the same software that they use.

No matter what you want to do with your PC, chances are Linspire has software you can use that will save you time, money, and hassle over other operating systems. In addition to having a number of programs pre-installed, Linspire offers you the most affordable way to get new software. The traditional method of getting software in the Microsoft Windows world is paying for each application you need. For Linux users, installing software usually means scouring the Internet for something that looks like it could be good, downloading several different packages, installing them with a series of commands, and hoping it works. One way costs you money, the other costs you time. With Linspire, you won't waste either.

For less than fifty dollars, Linspire users can get access to roughly 2,000 applications from the CNR Warehouse. In addition to this being incredibly low-priced, it's also incredibly easy. Don't waste time searching the web or looking through software boxes, just click and run. The warehouse is easily accessed with the CNR application that is integrated into the Linspire operating system. CNR lets you search for the specific application you want or browse through the warehouse aisles to find something that suits your needs. With CNR, you can look at screen shots, read descriptions, and install with a single click of your mouse button, saving you time and money.

## So Linspire saves me time and money, that's good. Is that all?

No. You see, Linspire is all about the marriage of cutting-edge technology with usability. An easier, less expensive operating system is a good start, but we want a better operating system. Since the time that XP came out, in 2001, there have been many technical innovations. And at Linspire, we don't think you should have to wait until 2007 to take advantage of them.

If you're like most people, chances are you have some friends that you chat with on AIM, some friends on Yahoo! Messenger, some on MSN, and even friends that use a different instant messaging program. It's getting to the point where you practically need a second screen just for all the different buddy lists and IM windows. With Linspire, you can simultaneously log onto all your IM accounts and view all of your buddies in one list. Then have all of your chats in one tabbed-window, freeing your screen from clutter so you don't lose track of an important conversation. But why stop at text-based communications? Our instant messenger lets you make free web-based worldwide phone calls.

By now you are probably familiar with the system slowdown dance. Leave your computer on for a couple of days in a row and it screeches to a halt. Make sure to set aside a day every month to defragment your hard drive (defragmenting moves data around on your hard drive because it is broken up, or fragmented), or else. Can you imagine if any other appliance in your house acted like that? What would it be like if you had to turn off your refrigerator occasionally or it wouldn't stay cold, or if you had to move around all your DVDs once a month or the DVD player wouldn't read them? Ridiculous, right? Well, why don't we think all these things are ridiculous with the PC as well? Because we have been conditioned to just accept slowdowns, freezes, crashes, and reboots as a way of life — but we shouldn't.

Because of Linspire's stability and security, you can leave your computer on for weeks - even months - at a time without worry. As for defragmenting — forget about it! Never defragment your computer again with Linspire. That's because Linspire's file system keeps itself from getting fragmented in the first place. So say goodbye to these unnecessary system slowdowns and freezes, and that aggravating blue screen that announces "your computer crashed and we lost your data." With Linspire, those frustrations that we've all had to just accept are now a thing of the past.

## So what's in store for the future?

Choice. Linspire has come a long way in three years. We've made an operating system that is just as good as its more expensive competition, and in many ways it's better. Expect that trend to continue. We work hard every day to make the world's best desktop operating system.

We're building technologies that make your life easier. From the creation of Lsongs (a music manager that lets you burn CDs, rip MP3s, download music, listen to music, share your music, and more), to the development of a licensed DVD player for watching commercial movies on Linux, we've been on the forefront of creating user-friendly software. With features like the free Internet-based phone calls of PhoneGaim, we're developing software that lets you do things with your computer that you couldn't before.

With the all-you-can-eat style of the CNR Warehouse and the family-friendly licensing that lets you install Linspire and CNR software on every computer in your home at no additional cost, we're implementing practices that put the consumer first.

We're taking a new approach at the technology business — putting you first, always asking what we can do to improve your life. With this as our approach, rather than the traditional "how can we make more money" stance that too many companies have taken, you can be assured that the future for Linspire means new, better, less expensive, more versatile software to make your life easier.

## Enjoy the book, and enjoy Linspire

I've given you just a glimpse of the innovations we've been working on at Linspire, and why we continue to innovate. This book will dive deeper into all the great features of Linspire and how to use them. You will probably find Linspire so easy to use that you won't need many of the sections of this book, but it's great to have as a reference.

If you've been desiring a computer that is more stable, more secure, more virus-resistant, easier to use, and more affordable, then you have come to the right place. With Linspire, choice has finally returned to the desktop market. Say goodbye to high prices and lack of innovation. Say goodbye to the constant barrage of spyware, viruses, popups, freezes, crashes, and the other maladies that have plagued your computing experience, and say hello to Linspire. Welcome to a world of choice, affordability, reliability, innovation, and ease-of use. Linspire is the operating system designed with you in mind.

# Table of Contents

# Chapter 5 Word Processing

# Chapter 6 Creating Spreadsheets

# Chapter 7 Creating Graphics & Slide Shows

# Chapter 8 Using Multimedia Programs

# Chapter 9 Connecting to the Internet

# Chapter 10 Installing Programs

# Chapter 11 Browsing the Internet

# Chapter 12 E-Mail

# Chapter 13 Instant Messaging

# Chapter 14 Home Networking

# Chapter 15 Getting Help

# Chapter 16 Printers

# Installing Linspire

Maybe it was just my inner geek developing, but I remember being so envious of the smart kids who got to skip a grade in primary school. For those of us who weren't deemed bright enough to jump grades, here's a free pass from me. If you purchased a Linspire computer with the operating system already installed, then you have my permission to skip ahead to the "Running Linspire for the First Time" section of this chapter. If you're still here it means that you've made the smart decision to install Linspire yourself on a new or existing system.

It wasn't that many years ago that the process of installing a Linux based operating system on your computer was a daunting task that could take hours, if not days. In fact, there used to be install parties on weekends where people would get together to help each other to get Linux installed and running properly. A lot has changed over the years and the installation of Linspire just involves a few clicks of your mouse button. In this chapter we'll explore the installation options, take you through the installation process and also explore LinspireLive!, an option for those hesitant to jump into the world of Linspire.

In this chapter we'll cover:

- Conducting a takeover installation
- Installing to a partition
- Running LinspireLive!

# Preparing for Installation

If you're a frequent flyer you know that before taking off the pilot goes through an intensive checklist to ensure that everything is ready for a safe and uneventful flight. The same is true for the Linspire installation process. There are several key points that you should understand before beginning the installation process. These include: understanding how to boot from a CD, creating partitions for your hard drive (this is optional), and ensuring your minimum system requirements are correct.

## Booting from CD

When a computer first starts, it looks to certain devices to give it instructions on what to load and how to begin. The order in which it looks to these devices is called the boot sequence. In most cases, your computer is pre-configured to first check for a CD from which to boot. If your system doesn't find a CD, it will then look to your hard drive for an operating system. If your computer doesn't automatically boot from the Linspire CD in the drive, you will need to change the boot sequence. You can find the boot sequence in the computer's BIOS (Basic Input Output System).

Although every computer is different, you can generally find instructions about accessing the BIOS from a splash screen that appears when you first start your computer. Typically this screen will indicate what key to press to enter the system BIOS, which is sometimes also called "setup." Once you are in the BIOS you can change the boot sequence so that your computer looks to your CD drive first. If you're having trouble changing the boot sequence for your computer, the Internet is a great resource for getting help. If you can access a computer with an Internet connection you can perform a Google search (www.google.com). In the Google search box, type the brand of your computer and the words "boot sequence." The web results will display instructions on changing the boot sequence for your computer.

## Creating Partitions

You can divide the hard drive on your computer into distinct sections called "partitions." Linspire lets you install the operating system either to the entire hard drive or to one of these partitions. Before you can install to a partition, you must first set it up correctly. Please keep in mind that you should be comfortable with creating partitions as you can inadvertently delete existing data on your computer. You can find instructions on creating hard drive partitions on the Internet, or as part of the documentation of your partitioning software.

## Minimum System Requirements

The final thing you need to do before starting the installation process is to ensure that your computer has enough power to run Linspire. Although it is possible to install the operating system on a machine that doesn't meet all of these requirements, it is not recommended. The minimum system requirements are as follows:

- 128 MB of RAM

- An 800MHz processor (or equivalent AMD processor)

- 4GB of available hard disk space

- A monitor with 1024 x 768 resolution

- CD-ROM or DVD drive, keyboard and mouse

- Linspire-compatible sound card and speakers or headphones (recommended)

- Ethernet card for Internet/LAN connectivity (recommended)

# Installing Linspire

To complete the installation process, you must answer a few simple questions in the Installation wizard. As you go through the wizard, you will have to make a decision whether you want to install the operating system to the hard drive, or want to install the operating system to a partition.

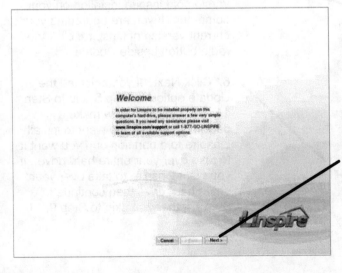

1. Insert the Linspire installation CD in your computer's CD drive and start your computer. After several moments a splash screen will appear. At this point you can press Enter on your keyboard or just wait, and after several seconds the installation process will continue.

2. Click Next. You'll advance to the next screen of the installation process.

*Be patient during the initial install stage. Depending on the speed of your computer and its components, it may take several minutes for the initial install screens to appear.*

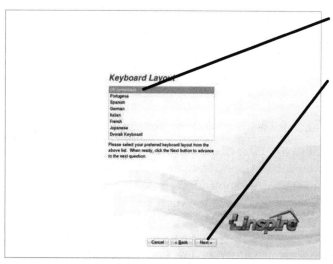

3.  Click your desired keyboard settings.  Your selection will be highlighted.

4.  Click Next.  You'll advance to the next step of the installation process.

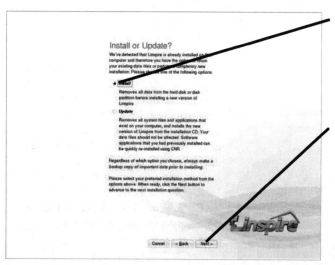

5.  Click the radio button beside Install, unless you already have a version of Linspire installed on your computer.  If you are upgrading your current version of Linspire, click the radio button beside Update.

6.  Click Next.  If you selected the Update option in Step 5 skip to Step 11.  You'll have to now make a decision whether you want to install Linspire to a partition or if you want it to take over your entire hard drive.  If you want Linspire to take over your entire hard drive then continue to Step 7, otherwise skip to Step 9.

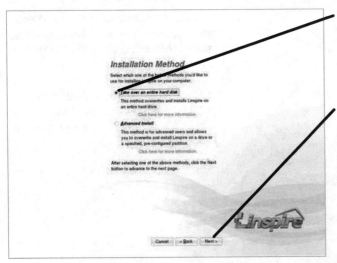

7.  Click the radio button beside Take over an entire hard disk. A little dot will appear in the circle after it has been selected.

8.  Click Next.  You'll advance to the next step of the installation process. Proceed to Step 11 as the next two steps deal with partition installations.

*If you are installing Linspire to a partition make sure that the partition has at least four gigabytes of space.  This will ensure you have enough space for both Linspire and your files.*

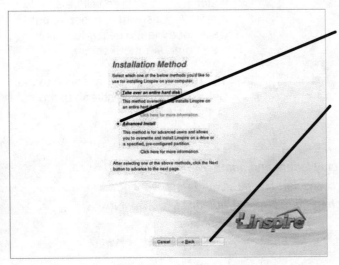

9.  Click the radio button beside Advanced Install.  A little dot will appear in the circle after it has been selected.

10.  Click Next.  You'll advance to the next step of the installation process.

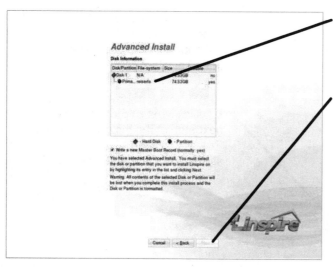

11.  Click the desired partition where you would like to install the operating system.  After you click the partition, it will be highlighted.

12. Click Next.  If you selected the "Update" installation option in Step 5 jump to Step 16.  Otherwise continue to Step 13.

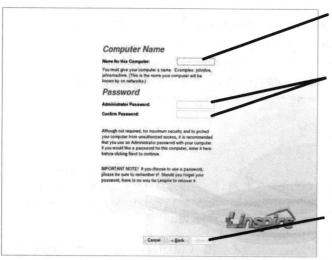

13.  Type a name for your computer. This is how your computer will be recognized on a network.

14.  Type a password in the Administrator and Confirm Password fields.  The password will appear as a series of stars, so that nobody watching your screen will be able to see it.  A password is optional, but it's a good idea to help you make your computer more secure.

15.  Click Next. You'll advance to the Setup Confirmation screen of the install wizard.

*Use only letters and numbers when naming your computer. Hyphens, underscores, and other characters cause problems if you want to network your computer.*

*Use a password that you are sure to remember as Linspire has no way of recovering it. It may be a good idea to write the password down and store it in a safe place.*

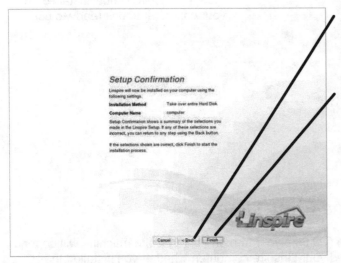

16. Click the Back button after reviewing the Setup Confirmation screen if there is anything that needs to be changed.

17. Click Finish. A dialog box will appear giving you a last chance to go back and make changes before the installation begins.

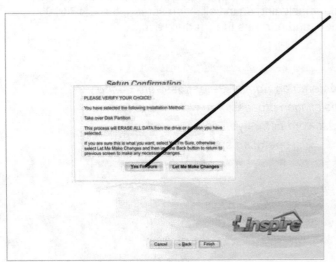

18. Click the Yes I'm Sure button. The installation process will begin. Various splash screens and a progress indicator will appear indicating what percentage of the installation is complete.

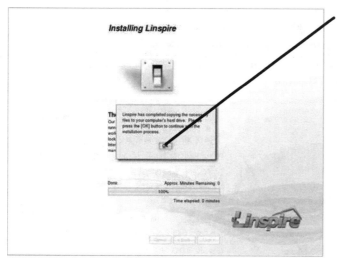

19. Click OK. Your computer will restart, and the CD will be ejected from the CD drive. Take the CD out when it is ejected then close the CD door and press the Enter key on your keyboard. It may take several minutes for the system to completely restart. Linspire is now installed on your computer and is ready to use.

# Running Linspire for the First Time

What you see on your screen the first time your turn on your Linspire machine will depend on several factors: who configured your Linspire computer; whether you installed the operating system yourself, or if your computer came pre-installed from the store. There are several screens that may appear including an initialization screen, the CNR trial membership screen, a tutorial video, and perhaps the Startup wizard.

*If you entered an Administrator password during the installation process, you will need to type that password before you can proceed into the operating system.*

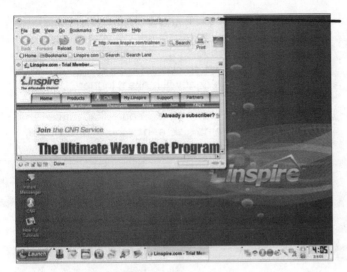

1. Click the "X" in the top right corner to clear the screen of any open windows.

# The Startup Wizard

The Startup wizard will run automatically the first time you launch your Linspire computer. If this wizard does not appear, do not panic. This simply means that whoever installed Linspire on your machine has completed the wizard for you. In any case, all of the configurations set by the Startup wizard can be adjusted at any time. You'll learn how to make these adjustments in the chapter entitled "Personalizing and Customizing Linspire."

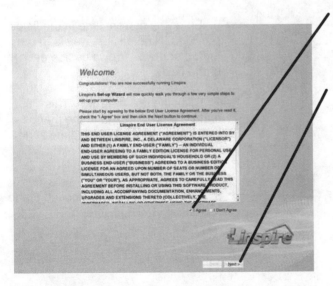

1. Click the check box beside the phrase "I Agree" after you' ve reviewed the license agreement. A check will appear in the box.

2. Click Next. You'll advance to the next screen of the wizard.

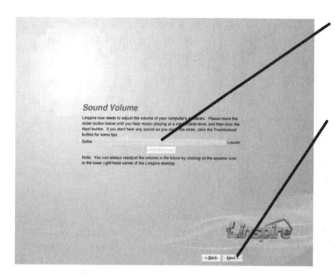

3. Click and drag the slider bar to adjust the volume of your system. Dragging the slider to the left will lower the volume and dragging it to the right will make it louder.

4. Click Next. You will advance to the next screen of the wizard where you can adjust the time and date settings.

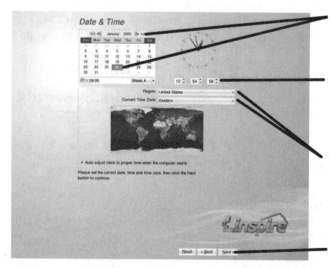

5. Click the correct date. You can adjust the month and year by clicking the arrows at the top of the calendar.

6. Enter the current time in the fields provided. The easiest way is to click the up or down arrows beside each of the fields.

7. Click the down arrows. This feature lets you expand the menus where you can adjust the time zone and region if they are not already correct.

8. Click Next. You will proceed to the Advanced Settings screen.

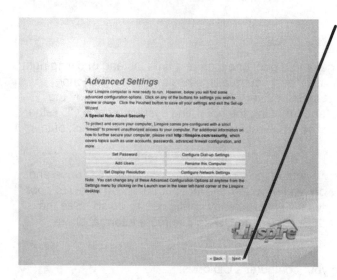

9.  Click Next at the Advanced Settings dialog box.  Alternatively you can click any of the boxes to adjust the settings.  Most of these settings will be discussed in detail later in the book.

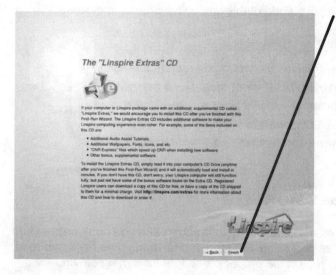

10.  Click Finish.  The wizard will close and you're now ready to explore the wonderful world of Linspire.  At this point a tutorial video may appear.  You can choose to watch this video, or click the "X" in the top right corner to close the tutorial.

# LinspireLive!

Are you one of those people who get into a pool one inch at a time instead of diving right in? For many people change is difficult, so if you're a little hesitant about exploring Linspire, you can take advantage of LinspireLive! LinspireLive! lets you to enjoy the benefits of Linspire on your computer by running the operating system off of a CD rather than installing it to your hard drive. The LinspireLive! CD is attached to the back of this book.

Running LinspireLive! is as simple as putting the CD into your computer's CD drive and restarting your system. The only work you have to do is let your computer know to boot from the CD rather than the hard drive if it is not already configured to do so. See the section earlier in the chapter entitled "Booting from CD" to see more information on accessing the BIOS.

1. Insert the LinspireLive! CD into your computer's CD drive.

2. Restart your computer. Depending on the operating system you are using, this action may involve using the Restart feature of the operating system or it may require turning off your computer then on again. Within moments the Linspire operating system will be loaded and you can begin exploring the world of this innovative operating system.

*LinspireLive! is a wonderful feature for testing Linspire, but it is not meant as a permanent solution. If you like what you see, you should install Linspire to your computer's hard drive.*

# Ending Your Linspire Session

I know...I know… you're too excited about using your computer and you don't want to turn it off. I'll give you five more minutes of playing, but then you have to come back and read the following section that instructs you on the proper procedure for turning off your computer.

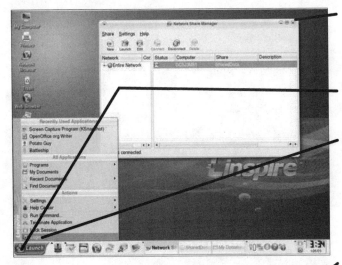

1.  Close any of your open applications by clicking the "X" in the top right corner.  You may be prompted to save your files.

2.  Click the Launch button. A menu will appear.

3.  Click Logout/Turn Off.  A dialog box will appear and will present you with several options.

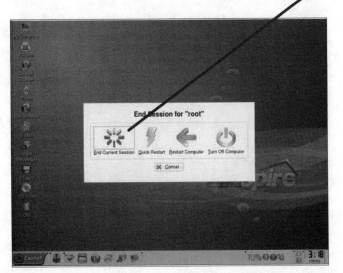

4.  Click one of the options, which include:

- End Current Session.  This logs you off but keeps your computer on.

- Quick Restart.  Lets you restart your computer quickly to allow a setting to take effect or resolve an issue. This usually takes seconds to complete.

- Restart Computer.  Lets you completely turn your computer off and on again.

- Turn Off Computer.  I'll give you three guesses as to what this does.

*Pressing the Ctrl, Alt and Delete key on the keyboard, all at the same time, will open the End Session dialog box.*

# Getting Acquainted with Linspire

**2**

You've either gone through the installation process, or you've turned on your pre-installed Linspire computer for the first time – now what? It's time to get acquainted with the operating system, learn your way around the key areas and start having some fun.

One of the best attributes of the Linspire operating system is that it is so easy to use. Whether you've never used a computer before or you are a seasoned veteran, you'll find that you'll be mastering Linspire in no time. On that note, if you are an experienced computer user, most of this chapter will be a review for you, so I suggest skimming over it. If on the other hand you're brand new to Linux, Linspire or computers in general, stick around and we'll discover the operating system together.

In this chapter we'll cover:

- Identifying the components of the user interface
- Getting around in Linspire
- Starting programs
- Managing open windows

# The User Interface

The term "user interface" is just fancy computer talk for what you see on your screen. The Linspire user interface is made up of a variety of components, each designed to make finding and executing programs easy.

# The Desktop

The desktop is the background area of the screen in Linspire. When you run programs, they run on top of the desktop. In Linspire the desktop is made up of a variety of components, each with their own special name and function.

### Desktop Icons

The desktop icons are the little pictures that appear along the left side of your screen. Each one of these icons has a different function, but in general when you double-click a desktop icon, the program associated with it will launch.   You can also rearrange, customize and delete icons based on your preferences.  You can find more on customizing icons in the next chapter entitled "Personalizing & Customizing Linspire."  For now, we will cover the icons that appear by default on the desktop.  By double-clicking these icons you can perform the following actions.  Note that the order of appearance of icons on your desktop may be slightly different from what you see here.

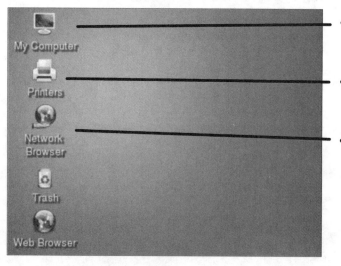

- My Computer. Lets you open a window where you can view the files on your computer.

- Printers. Lets you open a window so you can add, configure, or remove printers.

- Network Browser. Lets you open a window so you can view and configure computers on your network.

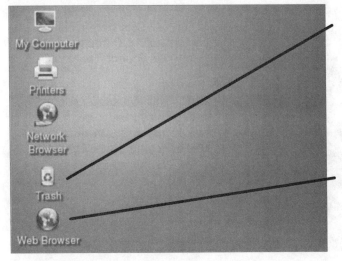

- Trash. When you delete a file on your computer, it is sent to the Trash. You can restore files that you have inadvertently deleted if the files have not yet been emptied from the Trash. More information on the Trash will be covered in the chapter entitled "File Management."

- Web Browser. Lets you launch the Linspire Internet suite so you can surf the Internet.

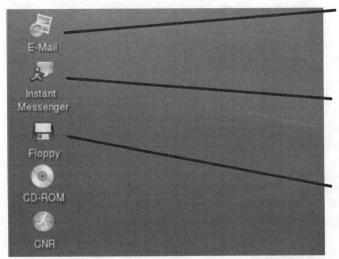

- E-Mail. Lets you launch the Linspire e-mail application (called the E-Mail Client) so you can send, receive, and manage your e-mail.

- Instant Messenger. Lets you communicate instantly with family, friends and coworkers. Double-clicking this icon will launch the Instant Messenger program.

- Floppy. Lets you access the files on any floppy disks you have inserted in your computer.

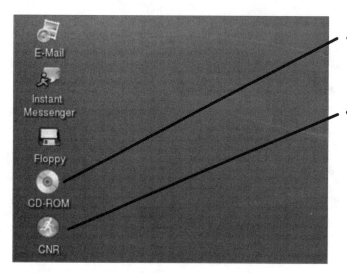

- CD-ROM. Lets you reveal the contents of a CD that has been inserted in your computer's CD drive.

- CNR. This is a subscription-based software service that makes installing software on your Linspire computer fast and easy.

*If you don't see an icon for a particular application that you would like to launch, don't worry. In the next chapter you'll learn to create an icon for any program.*

## The Panel

The Panel is the bar found at the bottom of the desktop that quickly allows you to access your applications. A handy feature of the Panel is that it remains visible regardless of the number of programs you have running. This feature is great for managing the programs you are running and for giving you access to applications at any time. Later in this chapter, we will describe in detail the four parts of the Panel. But right now lets look at an overview of what the parts of the Panel are and what they do.

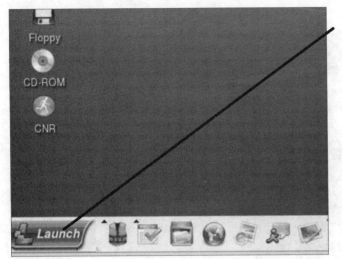

- Launch button. Lets you launch almost every program on your computer. From the Launch button you can start programs, configure your system, get help, or exit Linspire. The Launch menu that appears when you click the Launch button is composed of certain actions, all your applications and your recently accessed programs.

- Quick Launch bar. Lets you access applications instantly. The Quick Launch bar never gets obstructed by open programs and, unlike desktop icons, the icons on the Quick Launch bar only need to be clicked once to launch their respective programs.

- Taskbar. Lets you minimize, maximize, restore, close and switch between programs. All open programs are represented by an icon on the Taskbar.

- System Tray. Lets you configure certain elements of your Linspire computer. Among other things, it allows you to set and view the time and date, adjust the system volume and turn your computer off.

## The Quick Launch Bar

The Quick Launch bar allows you to launch programs with a single click of the mouse button. Unlike icons on your desktop, the Quick Launch bar is never hidden, so you can always access any application on that bar. By default, there are five icons on the Quick Launch bar, but you can add or remove icons as you see fit. More on customizing the Quick Launch bar can be found in the next chapter entitled "Personalizing & Customizing Linspire." In the section below, we will examine the five icons on the Quick Launch bar:

- File Manger. Lets you launch the File Manager, where you can manage the files and folders on your computer.

- Web Browser. Lets you start the Web Browser so you can surf the Internet. The Web Browser icon looks like a globe.

- E-Mail. Lets you launch the E-Mail Client application that will allow you to configure, send, receive and view e-mail messages.

- Instant Messenger. Lets you launch Instant Messenger, one of the most popular Internet features. Instant messaging allows you to chat directly with other computer users.

- Show desktop. Lets you minimize all the programs you have open so you can see the contents of the desktop.

# Launching Programs

In order to get anything accomplished with your computer, you will need to launch your software programs so that you can take advantage of what they have to offer. Linspire provides you with many ways to launch your programs.

## Launching Programs from Icons

Earlier in this chapter we discussed the different icons that appear on your desktop by default. These icons provide you with access to different applications on your computer.

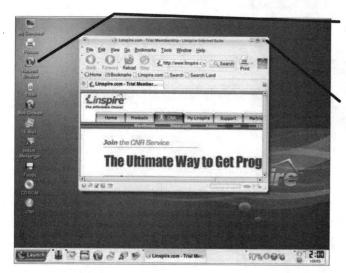

1. Double-click the Web Browser icon. This action will launch the Web Browser application that allows you to surf the Internet.

2. Click the "X" in the top right corner of an application to close it. This "X" is also referred to as the Close button.

*You may be asking yourself, "Why is there an icon flashing beside my cursor when I launch an application?" This flashing indicates that your computer is busy performing the requested task.*

## Launching Programs from the Launch Button

The Launch button gives you complete access to most of the applications on your computer. From the Launch button, you can select programs that are categorized based on their function. Although the Launch button gives you access to a variety of other tools, for now we will examine the steps to launch a program from this handy button.

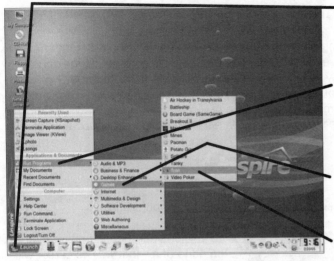

1.  Click the Launch button. The Launch menu will appear with a variety of operations or programs from which to choose.

2.  Click or just hover your mouse pointer over Run Programs. A submenu will appear with categories of the different programs that you have on your computer.

3.  Click Games. This feature will show you all of the programs that you have in this category.

4.  Click Tron. This action will launch the Tron program.  You can then close it by clicking the Close button.

## Launching Applications with the Quick Launch Bar

As we learned earlier, using the Quick Launch bar to launch programs has several advantages over using desktop icons.  The first benefit is that it only requires one click with the mouse button to launch a program.  The other advantage is that no matter how many programs you have running, you will still be able to view the Quick Launch bar.

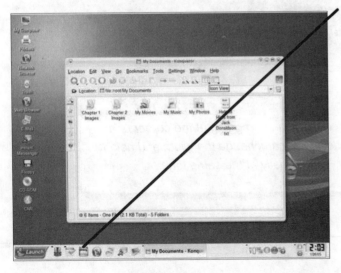

1.  Click the File Manager icon in the Quick Launch bar. The File Manager application will open.

# Working with Open Applications

It's very rare these days to be using a computer and only be running one program at a time. In today's fast-paced world, everyone is expected to multitask to get things done quicker, so it's quite possible that you will have multiple programs launched at any given time. The danger this poses is that you could find yourself in a world of mess and clutter if you don't know how to properly manage your open programs. The good news is that Linspire provides you with multiple ways to manipulate the appearance and location of your open applications.

## Resizing a Window

Resizing a program window in Linspire is as simple as clicking and dragging.

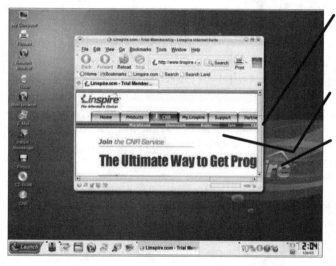

1. Position your mouse pointer over the edge of a window. The cursor will change into a double-sided arrow when you are over the correct spot.

2. Click and drag inward to reduce the size of the window.

3. Click and drag outward to increase the size of the window.

*By clicking and dragging at the corner of a window, you can change the width and height equally at the same time.*

## Minimizing and Restoring a Window

Minimizing a program simply means that you are putting it out of the way temporarily so that you can work in another program. When you minimize a program window, the program itself won't be affected by being minimized.

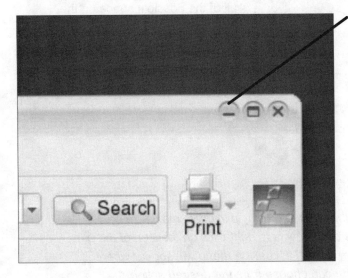

1.  Click the Minimize button. The window will no longer appear on the screen, but it can still be seen in the Taskbar.

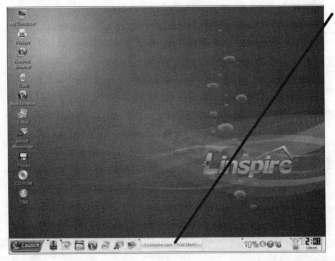

2.  Click an icon in the Taskbar. The program will restore to its previous state.

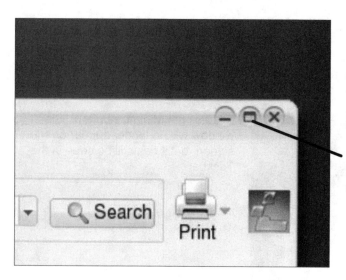

## Maximizing and Restoring a Window

The Maximize command allows you to resize a window so that it takes up all of the possible space on the desktop.

1. Click the Maximize button. This action will make the program as big as it can be on your screen.

*Another way to quickly minimize, maximize or restore a window is to right-click on the icon of the program in the Taskbar. A menu will appear where you can choose from the desired action.*

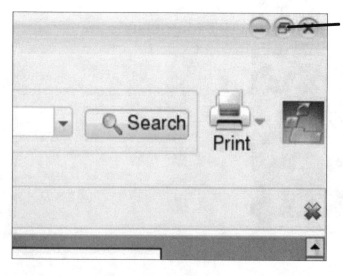

2. Click the Restore button. The window will return to its previous size.

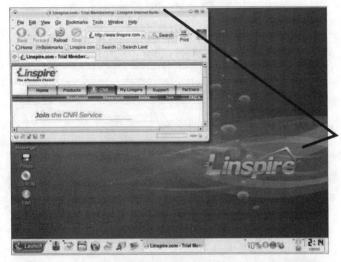

## Moving a Window

You can easily change the location of a window and reposition it anywhere on your screen. This action can be done with any window except one that has been maximized.

1. Click and drag a window from its Title bar to the desired location. As you drag, the window will move.

2. Release the mouse button. This action will let you reposition your window.

# Switching Between Programs

The Taskbar will contain a rectangular button representing each program that is currently running. You can use the Taskbar to quickly move between programs.

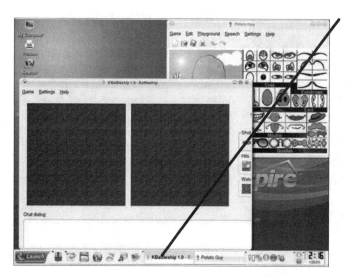

1. Click the icon representing a program in the Taskbar. This action will bring the selected program up in front of all other programs that you are running.

*You can hold down the Alt key and then press the Tab key to toggle between open programs.*

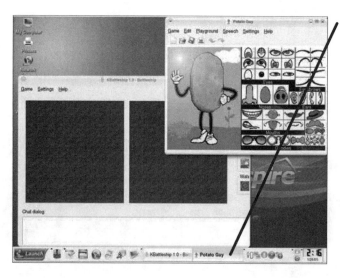

2. Click another program icon in the Taskbar. The program that you have just selected will now appear in front of your previously selected program.

# Cleaning Windows

Imagine being able to clean and organize your entire house with one click of a button. While that technology may not be in homes for years to come, it is available in Linspire. You can clean up and organize your open windows in seconds.

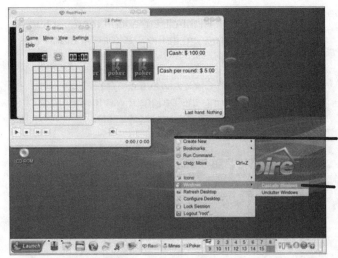

## Cascading Windows

Cascading your windows will organize them so that they overlap one another, but the Title bar of each open application will be visible in cascading order.

1. Right-click in any blank area of your desktop. A menu will appear.

2. Click Windows | Cascade Windows. Your open windows will now overlap with all of their Title bars exposed.

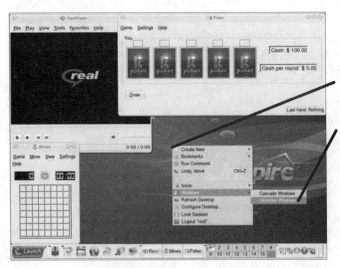

## Uncluttering Windows

This feature will evenly space out all of your open windows.

1. Right-click in any blank area of your desktop. A menu will appear.

2. Click Windows | Unclutter Windows. Your open windows will now be spaced out across the available room on the desktop.

# Always On Top

Sometimes you may want a program window to remain on top of all other windows regardless of whether or not you are currently working in that program. A good example of this would be when watching a video on the computer. Regardless of which program you are working in, you'd want the video to remain on top so that it is unobstructed.

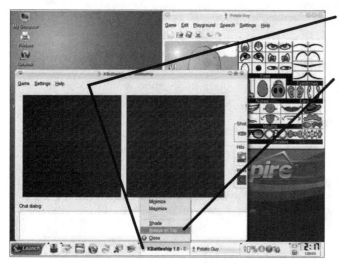

1. Right-click the icon representing a program in the Taskbar. A menu will appear.

2. Click Always on Top. This will bring the program window in front of all others.

3. Repeat Steps 1 and 2 to remove this feature.

# Working with Menus

Across the top of most programs you will find a menu bar that gives you access to the different commands within a program. The commands can be accessed in a variety of ways.

## Selecting Menu Items with the Mouse

Selecting a menu command is simply a matter of clicking on a menu item and then selecting a subsequent command.

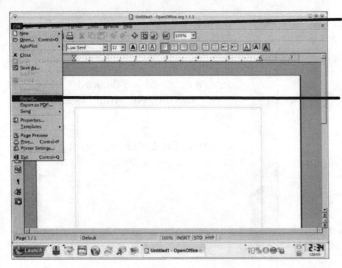

1.  Click File on the menu bar in an open application. The File menu will open, displaying commands that fall under that category.

2.  Click the desired command. That command will now be executed.

*Depending on the program you are using, you may be able to bring up a menu of commands by right-clicking with your mouse in a blank area of the screen.*

## Selecting Menu Items with a Keyboard

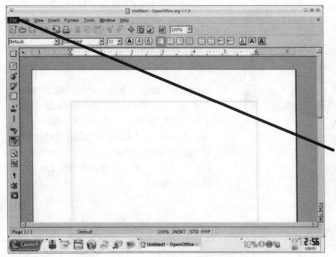

Another approach for selecting menu items is to use your keyboard. This can save you the hassle of having to switch between the keyboard and mouse if you are already typing within a program.

1.  Press the Alt key on your keyboard. The first category in the menu bar is highlighted. You can now press the right or left arrow keys on your keyboard to navigate across the menu bar.

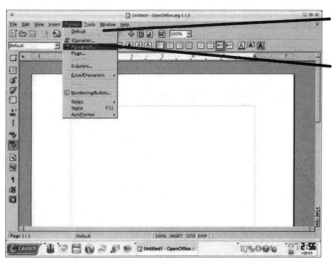

2. Press the down arrow. This will expand the currently selected menu.

3. Press the down arrow again until you've reached the desired command that you would like to execute.

4. Press the Enter key. The command you selected will be executed.

## Identifying Menu Items

When you opened an item on the menu bar, you may have noticed that some of the menu items have little markings beside them or that they seem to be grayed out. Each one of these little symbols has a different meaning.

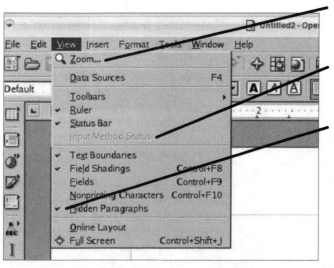

• Three Dots. This indicates that a dialog box will open when this command is executed.

• Dimmed Command. This indicates that the command is currently unavailable.

• Check Mark. This indicates that the option is currently selected. If you click a menu option that already has a check mark beside it, the menu option will be turned off and the check mark will be removed.

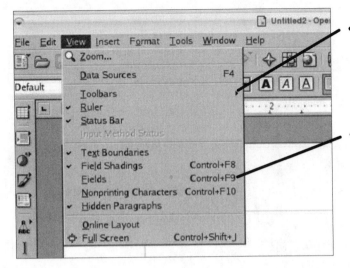

- Triangle. Indicates that there is a submenu associated with this command. By clicking or just hovering over this command with the mouse pointer, you will be able to view the submenu.

- Keystrokes. A series of words and letters beside a menu command indicates the keystrokes necessary to execute that command. For example, if it says Control+F8 beside a menu command, pressing the Ctrl key on your keyboard and the F8 key at the same time will execute that command.

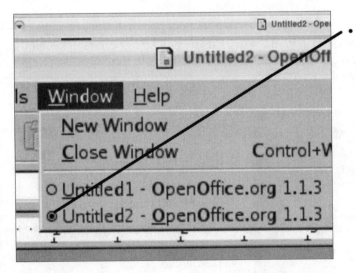

- Dot. This indicates that the option is currently selected. Unlike a check mark, a dot indicates that only one selection can be chosen at any given time.

# Scrolling

When there is more information within a window than can be displayed, scroll bars will appear. Scroll bars allow you to move through a window either horizontally or vertically so that you can see all of its contents.

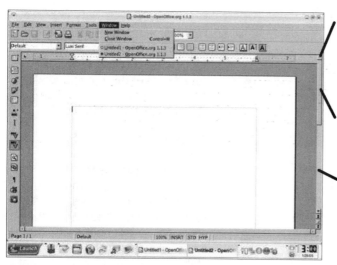

1.  Click a scroll arrow to either move the contents of the window up or down.  Each time you click an arrow, the contents will move up or down by one increment.

2.  Click and drag on the scroll box. The contents of the screen will move as you are dragging.

3.  Click anywhere along the scroll bar. The window will jump to a location between where you clicked and its current location.

# Terminating Programs

It has happened to all of us at one time or another.  For some reason a program freezes and we are unable to continue working in it.  If we were using any other operating system we would probably have to restart our computer.  Linspire allows us to terminate an application without having to reboot the system.

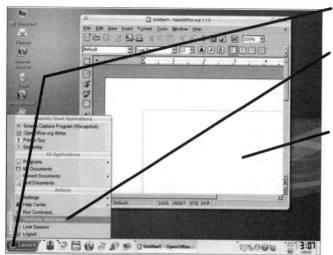

1.  Click the Launch button. The Launch menu will appear.

2.  Click Terminate Application. The Terminate a Frozen Application dialog box will appear, and your cursor will change.

3.  Click anywhere on the frozen application. The frozen application will terminate.

# Personalizing & Customizing Linspire

Imagine what kind of a world it would be if everyone had to drive the same car, wear the same clothes, watch the same shows and eat the same meals. Our individuality is of extreme importance to us, so it's understandable why Linspire offers so many customization options when it comes working in the operating system.

Since everyone works a little differently, Linspire allows you to change the look and feel of your computer to suit your individual tastes. From backgrounds to screen savers to icons to screen size Linspire gives you the ability to make the operating system your own. Not only can Linspire be personalized, but it offers a variety of unique tools that allow you to control the way in which you work.

In this chapter we'll cover:

- Changing backgrounds
- Selecting screen savers
- Manipulating icons
- Working with virtual desktops

**3**

# Changing the Wallpaper

The easiest way to personalize the look of your computer is to change the background image of the desktop. This background is also known as the "wallpaper." For the background, you can select from a variety of images, create a customized background, use one of your favorite photos, or even run a slide show.

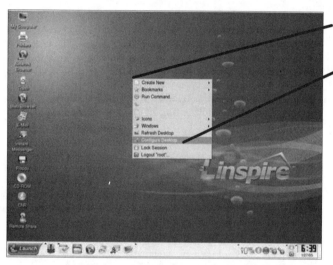

1. Right-click any blank area of the desktop. A menu will appear.

2. Click Configure Desktop... The Configure - Desktop dialog box will open to let you configure different elements of your desktop.

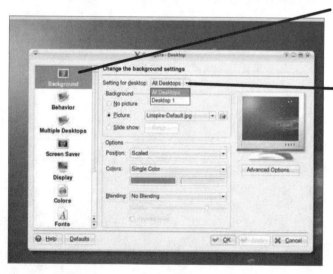

3. Click the Background icon if it is not already selected. This action will bring you to the area where you can control the look of your desktop.

4. Click the arrow beside "Setting for desktop:" and pick a specific virtual desktop where you can apply your setting. Alternatively you can select All Desktops to apply the same setting to each virtual desktop. You'll be learning more about virtual desktops later in this chapter.

You must now decide what type of background you would like: a picture, a slide show or a colored background.

## Selecting a Pre-Installed Wallpaper

Linspire comes with a variety of different images from which you can select.  Before proceeding make sure you have followed Steps 1 - 4 in the "Changing the Wallpaper" section earlier.

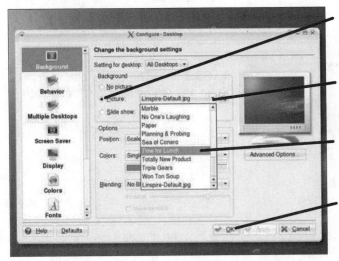

1.  Click the radio button beside Picture: if it is not already selected. A dot should be in the circle.

2.  Click the drop-down arrow. This action will display a list of backgrounds that come with Linspire.

3.  Click the desired wallpaper. A preview of the wallpaper will appear in the window.

4.  Click the OK button to finalize the background changes.

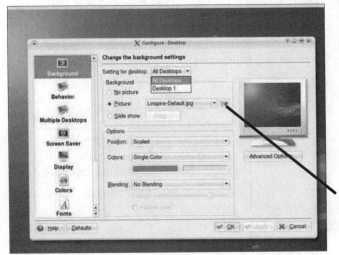

## Selecting Your Own Photos for the Wallpaper

Nothing personalizes a desktop more than a picture of your family, vacation, pets, or any other image from your personal collection. Linspire makes it easy to add your own pictures to the desktop.  Before proceeding make sure you have followed Steps 1 - 4 in the "Changing the Wallpaper" section.

1.  Click the Browse button.  A dialog box will open allowing you to navigate your computer for the desired image.

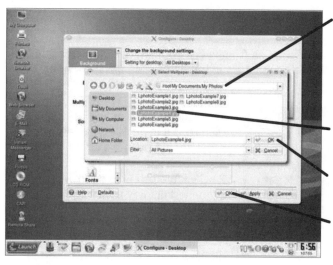

2. Navigate to the directory that contains the image you would like to use as your wallpaper. If you are unclear on how to navigate through your folders, see the chapter entitled "File Management."

3. Click the picture file you would like to use. It will be highlighted.

4. Click OK. The dialog box will close and your picture will be loaded.

5. Click the OK button to finalize the background changes.

## Changing the Wallpaper Colors

If you prefer to have a simple colored background rather than an image, Linspire gives you that option. You can have up to two different colors in your background and those colors can be applied in a variety of patterns. Before proceeding make sure you have followed Steps 1 - 4 in the "Changing the Wallpaper" section.

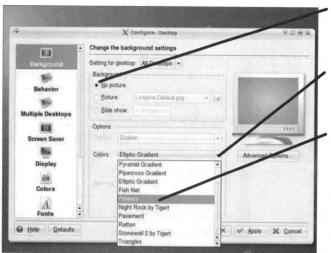

1. Click the radio button beside No picture. A dot will appear in the circle.

2. Click the drop-down arrow beside Colors. A list of different patterns that can be applied will appear.

3. Click the desired pattern. A preview of your colored pattern will appear in the monitor icon in the dialog box. If you want just a solid-color background select the Single Color option.

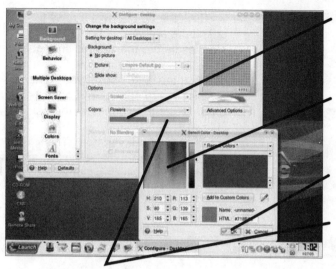

4. Click the first color box. The Select Color - Desktop dialog box will open, allowing you to change the first color in your pattern.

5. Click the desired color or enter a specific value for your color. A preview of the selected color will appear.

6. Click OK. The first color will be selected.

7. Repeat Steps 4 - 6 with the second color box to adjust its color. You can then click OK to finalize the changes.

## Creating a Slide Show as a Background

Variety is the spice of life, so why have just one background? You can create a slide show of pictures that you've selected that will continuously change the background. You can select which pictures to use, how they transition from one to the next, and how often they should change. Make sure you have followed Steps 1 - 4 in the "Changing the Wallpaper" section before proceeding.

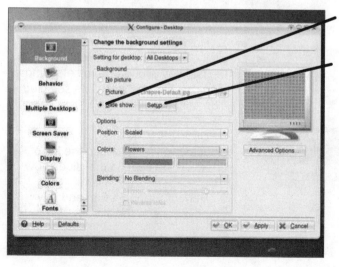

1. Click the radio button beside Slide show:. A dot will appear in the circle.

2. Click the Setup button. The Setup Slide Show - Desktop dialog box will open.

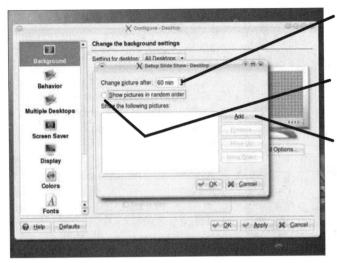

3.  Click the up or down arrows to adjust the amount of time that elapses before the images change.

4.  Click the check box if you want the pictures to appear in random order rather than one after the next.

5.  Click the Add... button. This feature will open a dialog box where you can select which pictures you'd like to use for your slide show.

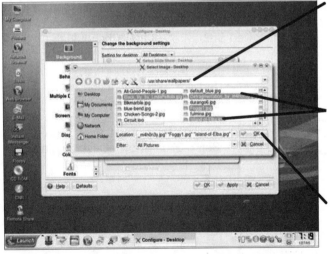

6.  Navigate to the directory that contains the images you would like to use in your slide show. If you are unclear on how to navigate through your folders, see the chapter entitled "File Management."

7.  Hold down the Ctrl key as you click different images. Holding down the Ctrl key allows you to select more then one file at a time. The selected files will be highlighted.

8.  Click OK. The images you selected will be added to the list of photos to be used in the slide show.

9.  Repeat Steps 5 - 8 to add any other images to the list.

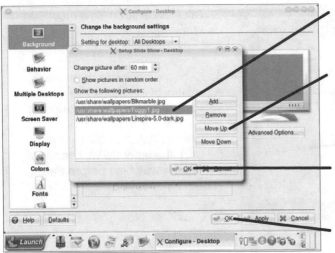

10. Click any photo in your list. The photo will be highlighted and several buttons will now be activated.

11. Click the Move Up or Move Down button to change the order of the selected photo. Alternatively, you can also press the Remove button to take a photo off the list.

12. Click OK. The dialog box will close and your wallpaper slide show will now be configured.

13. Click OK to finalize the background changes.

## Selecting Screen Savers

It used to be that computer monitors required screen savers to avoid an image being permanently burned into the monitor. Modern-day monitors don't have this issue, but screen savers still remain popular. Linspire comes with a variety of very creative screen savers from which you can choose.

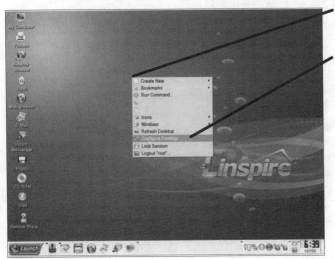

1. Right-click any blank area of the desktop. A menu will appear.

2. Click Configure Desktop... The Configure - Desktop dialog box will open, allowing you to configure different elements of your desktop.

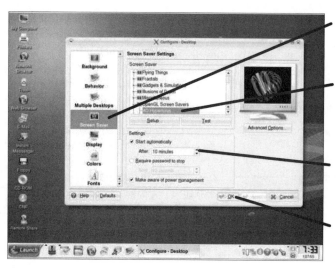

3. Click the Screen Saver icon. You can now select and adjust the settings for your screen saver.

4. Click the desired screen saver. A preview of the screen saver you selected will appear in the monitor icon in the dialog box.

5. Click the up or down arrows to adjust the wait time before the screen save begins.

6. Click OK. Now you've accepted the changes you've made to the screen saver settings.

# Adjusting the Panel

By default the Panel appears at the bottom of the screen, but if you prefer, it can be moved or resized to fit your preference. You can also change its size and length.

1. Right-click any blank area in the Taskbar. A menu will appear.

2. Click Configure Panel. The Configure - Panel dialog box will open.

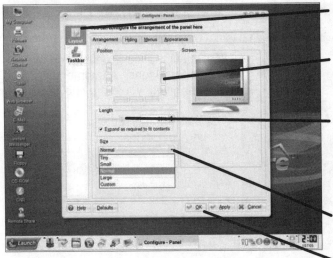

3. Click the Layout button if it is not already selected.

4. Click one of the position boxes to change where on the screen the Panel will appear.

5. Click and drag the slider to adjust the length of the Panel. As you drag, a preview of the look of the adjusted Panel will appear in the monitor icon in the dialog box.

6. Click the size drop-down button and select a size for your Panel.

7. Click OK, the dialog box will close and the changes will take effect.

# Working with Icons

Icons represent a convenient way to launch your programs and gain access to your files. Icons can actually act as double-edged swords because if you don't manage them properly, they can cause clutter, confusion and an outright mess.

## Arranging Desktop Icons

I'm sure you've got people like this at your office, and perhaps you might even be one of these people. You go by their computer screens and see dozens of icons scattered on their desktops. If you're the type of person who needs to access files and programs from your desktop, here's a quick way to keep your screen looking organized.

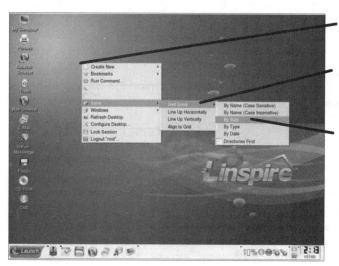

1. Right-click any blank area of the desktop. A menu will appear.

2. Select the Icons option and then select Sort Icons. A submenu will appear giving you more choices.

3. Click the desired method for sorting your icons.

*You can also manually sort or move your icons simply by clicking and dragging them to the desired location on your desktop.*

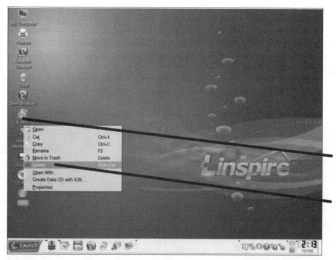

## Removing an Icon

The truth is that there are only a few programs that you use most of the time, so why have extra icons cluttering your screen? Even if you delete an icon you can always go back and recreate it.

1. Right-click the icon you want to delete. A menu will appear.

2. Click Delete. The icon will be removed from the desktop. If a Delete dialog box appears, click the Delete button to confirm the deletion.

# Changing an Icon's Appearance

If you don't like the look of a particular icon, you can change its appearance.

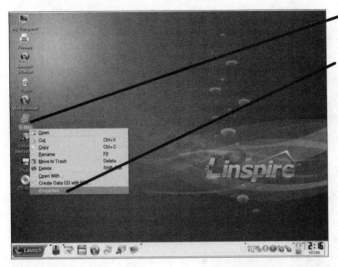

1. Right-click the icon you want to change. A menu will appear.

2. Click Properties. A dialog box will open where you can adjust its appearance.

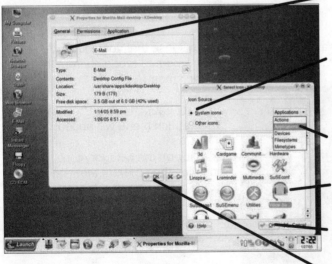

3. Click the icon in the top left corner of the dialog box. The Select Icon dialog box will open.

4. Click the radio button beside the desired source of icon you would like to see. A list of icons that fall under that source will appear.

5. Click the drop-down menu and select a category of icons to view.

6. Click a desired icon. It will be selected.

7. Click the OK button. The new icon will appear in the dialog box.

8. Click the OK button. The new icon will appear on the desktop replacing the old.

## Changing the Name of an Icon

You can change the name of any of the icons on your desktop, with the exception of some system icons like the Trash.

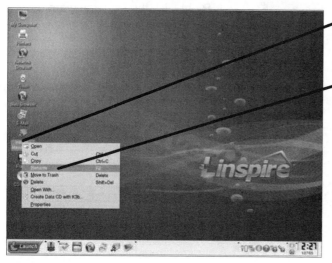

1. Right-click on the icon that you would like to change. A menu will appear.

2. Click Rename. The Properties dialog box will open.

3. The name of the icon will now be highlighted and you can type a new name.

4. Press the Enter key on your keyboard when you have finished renaming the icon.

## Creating an Icon

We all know the benefits of using an icon, so it just makes sense that you should be able to create them for any application. You can do this by clicking and dragging from the Launch menu.

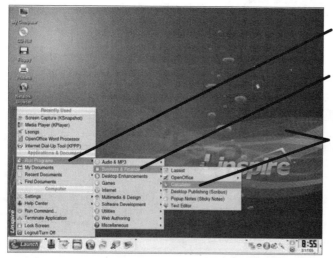

1. Click Launch | Run Programs. The Launch menu will appear.

2. Click on the category that contains the program that you would like to add to the desktop.

3. Click and drag the desired program to the desktop.

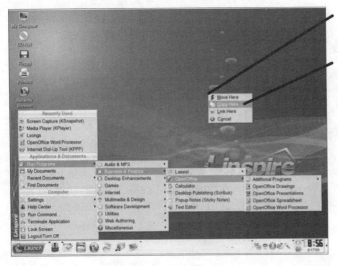

4.  Release the mouse button and a menu will appear.

5.  Click Copy Here.  An icon for the program you dragged will appear on the desktop.

*Once you have created a desktop icon you can move it, sort it and change its appearance like any other icon.*

## Adding Icons to the Quick Launch Bar

Any program can be added to the Quick Launch bar so that it can be accessed at any time with just one click of the mouse button.

1.  Click the Taskbar Menu button.  It is a little black arrow at the end of the Quick Launch bar.  A menu will appear.

2.  Click Panel Menu | Add | Application Button.  A list of different categories of buttons will appear.

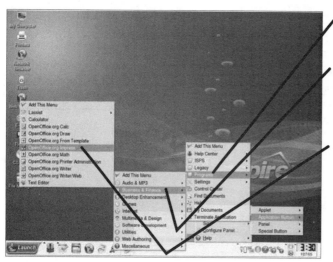

3. Click Programs. A list of different types of programs will appear.

4. Click the category that falls under the programs you want to add. A list of programs in that category will appear.

5. Click the name of the program whose icon you'd like to add to the Quick Launch bar. The icon for the program you selected will now be a part of the Quick Launch bar.

You can remove an icon from the Quick Launch bar by right-clicking on it and then selecting the Remove (button name) command.

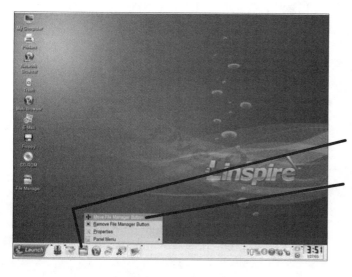

## Repositioning Quick Launch Icons

Icons on the Quick Launch bar can be repositioned to customize the way in which you work.

1. Right-click the icon that you'd like to move. A menu will appear.

2. Click Move (button name). As you move your mouse pointer across the Quick Launch bar the icon will move with it.

3. Click once, and the icon will be in its new location.

*You can click and drag any icon from the Quick Launch bar to the desktop. When you release the mouse button a menu will appear and you'll have the option to copy or move the icon.*

# Virtual Desktops

Would you believe me if I told you that your Linspire computer can actually be twenty different computers in one? Maybe that's a bit of a stretch, but Linspire does allow you to have up to twenty different desktops. While you can only view one desktop at a time, there are many reasons why virtual desktops can be advantageous. Virtual desktops are particularly beneficial to those who like to keep dozens of icons on their desktops. Using virtual desktops, you could create one desktop for games, another desktop for spreadsheets, and another for documents. You can also use virtual desktops when installing programs or to download large files off the Internet because you can work in one desktop while the other desktop is busy. What you do with your virtual desktops is up to you, just know that Linspire makes them easy to use and configure.

## Creating Virtual Desktops

By default there is just one desktop set up for you when you first install Linspire. If you want to take full advantage of the virtual desktop features, you can set up a total of twenty different desktops.

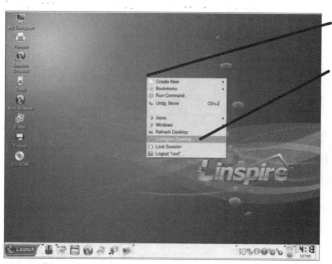

1. Right-click any blank area of the desktop. A menu will appear.

2. Click Configure Desktop… The Configure - Desktop dialog box will open to let you to configure different elements of your desktop.

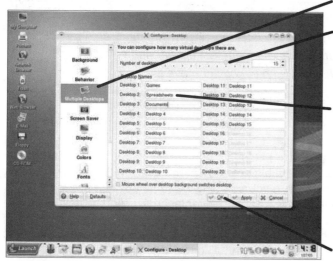

3. Click the Multiple Desktops icon.

4. Click and drag the slider to the right. As you drag, the number of desktops will increase, up to a maximum of twenty.

5. Type a name for any or all of the virtual desktops you've set up. To change a desktop name, double-click the existing name and then begin typing. Although you don't have to give your desktops a name, it makes it easier to manage them if you do.

6. Click OK. Your virtual desktops will now be configured.

*Follow the same procedures above to remove virtual desktops. Drag the slider mentioned in Step 4 all the way to the left until the number of desktops is down to one.*

## Accessing Virtual Desktops

To access your virtual desktops you will need to set up an applet (a mini program). Once this is set up you will have instant access to your desktops. The applet we are going to use is called the "Pager" option. This feature allows you to see a series of buttons, each button representing a virtual desktop.

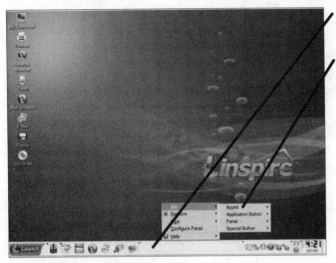

1. Right-click any empty area on the Taskbar. A menu will appear.

2. Click Add | Applet. A list of different Applets will appear.

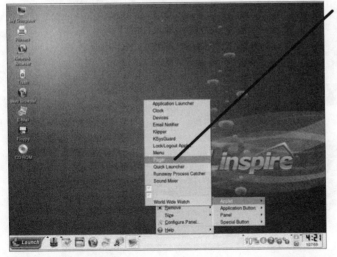

3. Click Pager. Several buttons, each representing one of your virtual desktops that you set up earlier, will appear on the Taskbar.

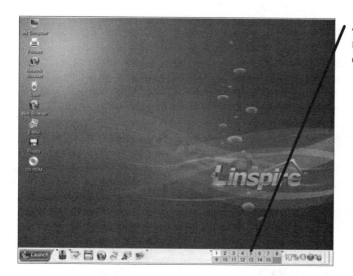

4. Click on the desired desktop number to toggle between the different desktops.

## Sending Applications to Desktops

Say for example you are watching a video on your computer, and you want to ensure that you can see that video on any desktop that you switch to. You can pin down an application so that it appears on every desktop. Alternatively you can send an application to any other desktop.

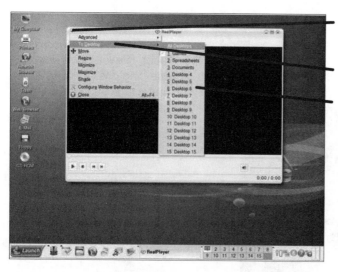

1. Click the triangle in the upper left corner of any open application.

2. Click the To Desktop option.

3. Click the All Desktops option to have your application appear in any of your virtual desktops.
Alternatively, pick any desktop where you would like to send this program.

# Adjusting the Date

During the Startup wizard you were prompted to enter the current date to be displayed on your computer. You can adjust the date that was entered at any time using the system tray.

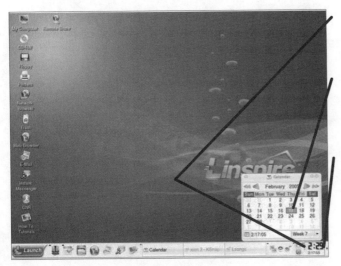

1. Click the clock in the system tray. A calendar will appear from which you can specify the date.

2. Click today's date. It will be highlighted. You can also use the arrows at the top of the calendar to toggle between days and months.

3. Click the clock again to hide the calendar. The date you entered will now take effect.

# Adjusting the System Volume

You can adjust the master control for your computer's volume from the system tray.

1. Click the Volume icon in the system tray. A volume slider will appear.

2. Click and drag the slider up or down to adjust the volume level.

3. Click the Volume icon again to close the slider. The master volume will now be set.

# File Management

The ability to manage your files is of paramount importance when working on your computer. Almost everything contained in your computer, whether it's a document, a spreadsheet, a photo, a song or an e-mail, is stored as a file. Even the programs that you run are made up of different files. In fact, most computers have literally thousands of different files.

Keeping track of these files would be a complete nightmare if you didn't have a proper filing system, and it just so happens that Linspire has an excellent one. Files are categorized into folders (sometimes called directories) and are placed into logical categories. If you have experience with other operating systems like Windows, you'll find that the file structure in Linspire is a little different, but you'll get the hang of it in no time.

In this chapter we'll cover:

- Navigating your computer for files
- Using the File Manager
- Creating, editing and deleting files
- Searching your computer

# The File Manager

Think of the File Manager as a very large virtual filing cabinet. Your computer is made up of thousands of files, and the File Manger allows you to access those files in a logical fashion. Just like in a real filing cabinet, the files in your computer are contained in folders.

1. Click the File Manager icon from the Quick Launch bar. The File Manager will launch. Alternatively you can double-click the My Computer icon on the desktop to launch a simplified version of the File Manager. Although simplified, it still provides most of the functionality of the File Manager. All of the file management techniques found in this book can be done using either version of the File Manager.

*Another option for launching the File Manager is to double-click the My Computer icon on the desktop.*

# Viewing Files

The File Manager gives you a graphical representation of all of the files on your computer. You can adjust this graphical representation to suit your particular preference. For example, you can view your files as different sized icons, choose to view the details of your files, view your files in columns, or change the view structure. The type of view you select will depend on your goals and preferences.

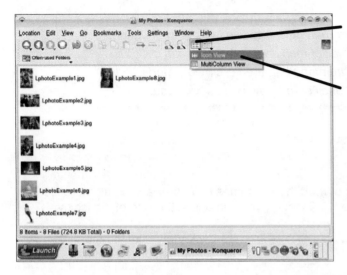

1.  Click and hold the first View button.  A list of view options will appear.

2.  Click on the desired view option. Your choices include:

*   Icon View.  This view displays your files or folders as icons, with the name of the file or folder beneath the icon.

*   MultiColumn View.  This is almost identical to the Icon View except that it sorts your icons into tidy columns.

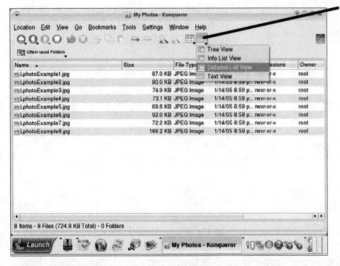

3.  Click and hold the second View button.  The following list of additional view options will appear from which you can click:

*   Tree View.  This option displays the contents of your computer in a tree diagram.  You can expand and retract different folders to reveal or hide their contents.

*   Info List View.  This view shows your files and folders as a list.

*   Detailed List View.  This view displays additional information on your files like their size, type, permission and so on.

*   Text View.  This view is very similar to the Detailed List View except the Text View displays no icons and there is a "/" in front of every folder name.

*Rather than having to use two different buttons to see all of the view modes, you can click View from the menu bar, then click View Mode. A list of all of the view modes will appear.*

## Changing Icon Size

If you are finding it difficult to see or read the file names or if you want to see more files on the screen when navigating in the File Manger, you can adjust the size of the icons.

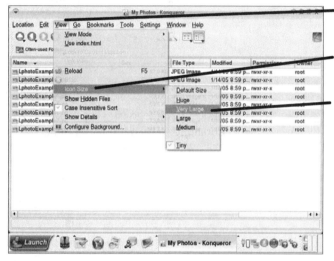

1. Click View from the menu bar. A list of commands will appear.

2. Click Icon Size. A list of different sizes will appear.

3. Click the desired size. The icons in the File Manager will change to the size you selected.

# Navigating Files

When you start the File Manager, you'll be taken to the location called "Home." Think of the Home screen as your home base, a location that you can return to at any time, no matter where you've navigated to on your computer. Starting from the Home screen lets you quickly move to different locations across your computer. The File Manger provides you with a variety of navigation tools so getting around the contents of your computer is a breeze. If you're wondering what some of the folders are for, consult the section later in this chapter entitled "Understanding Linspire Folders."

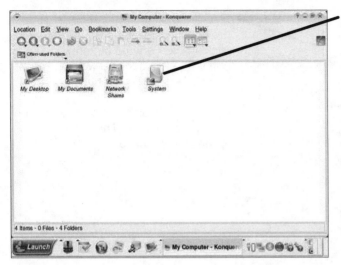

1. Double-click the System folder. The contents of your computer will be revealed.

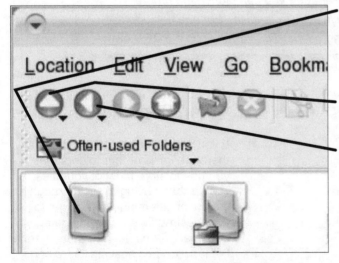

2. Double-click any folder. The contents of that folder will appear on the screen. Within a folder you will typically find other folders, files or both.

3. Click the Up button to move up a level in the hierarchy.

4. Click the Back button. This will take you back to the screen you previously viewed. You can continue clicking the Back button until you get to the point where you started navigating.

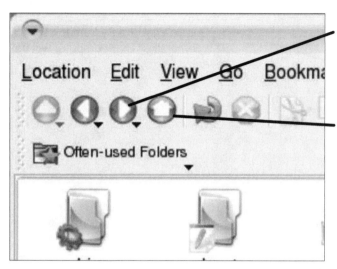

5.  Click the Forward button.  If you previously clicked the Back button, clicking the Forward button will take you to the location you were at before you clicked the Back button.

6.  Click the Home button at any point in your navigation.  This will take you to the Home location.

*By double-clicking on any file in the File Manager, you can launch the program associated with that file.  For example, double-clicking on an PDF file will open a PDF Viewer.*

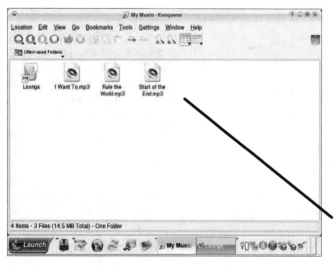

## Using Bookmarks

If you are like most computer users, there are three or four folders that you use to store most of your files. Rather than having to click through a variety of different folders to get to your desired files, you can use a bookmark.  A bookmark remembers the location of a specific folder and lets you jump to that location instantly.

1.  Navigate to the location for which you would like to create a bookmark.

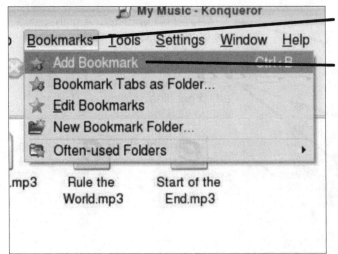

2. Click Bookmark. The Bookmark menu will appear.

3. Click Add Bookmark. A button will appear on the toolbar that you can now use to quickly jump to that location. Alternatively click Ctrl+B at any time to create a bookmark.

4. Repeat Steps 1 - 4 to add any other bookmarks.

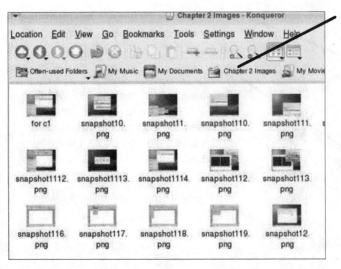

5. Click any of your bookmark buttons on the toolbar to quickly jump to those locations.

# Selecting Files and Folders

Before you can do any type of file management like copying, moving or deleting files and folders, you must first select the ones that you would like to manipulate. There are several different methods you can use to select individual or multiple files and folders.

1.  Click a file or folder. A highlighted file or folder indicates that you have selected it.

2.  Hold down the Ctrl key and click any other files or folders. They too will now be selected.

3.  Click any blank area of the screen. The files and folders will no longer be selected.

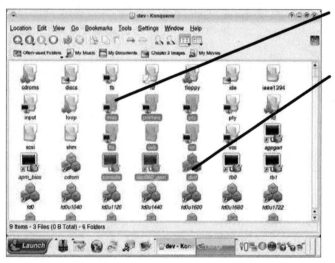

4.  Click a file or folder. A highlighted folder indicates that you have selected it.

5.  Hold down the Shift key and click a file elsewhere in the window. All the files in the same rows and columns between the original file you clicked and the last file you clicked will now be selected.

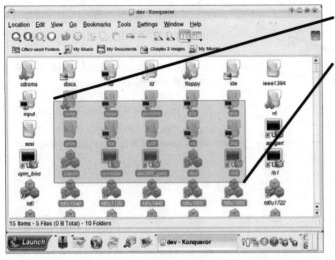

6. Position the mouse pointer in a blank area between files.

7. Click and drag diagonally. As you drag a marquee will appear. The files and folders that the marquee touches will be selected.

## Copying and Pasting Files

Copying and pasting are the most common tasks performed with files and folders. When you cut or copy a file or folder it is sent to a virtual clipboard. It can then be pasted to any location that you specify. Here we'll go through one of the quickest methods to copy.

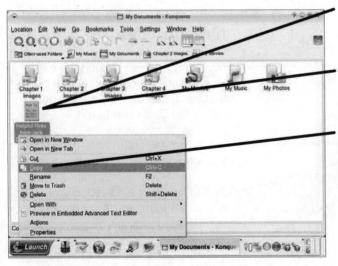

1. Select the file(s) or folder(s) that you would like to copy using one of the selection methods.

2. Right-click on the selection you would like to copy. A menu will appear.

3. Click Copy. The selection will be copied to the clipboard. Pressing Ctrl+C on your keyboard also enables the Copy command.

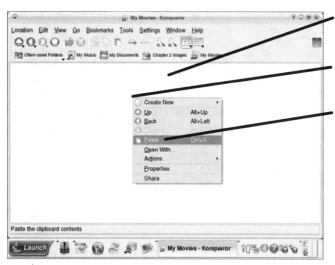

4. Navigate to the location where you want to paste the file.

5. Right-click in any blank area of the screen. A menu will appear.

6. Click Paste. The selection will be pasted to this location. Alternatively you can press Ctrl+V to paste the file.

*When copying and pasting a folder, both the folder and all of its contents will be pasted to the new location.*

## Moving Files

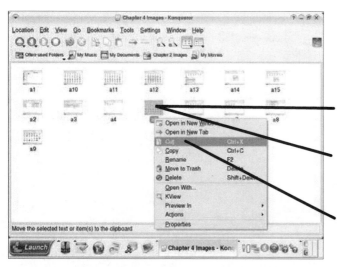

Moving a file works much the same as copying, the only exception being that you'll use the Cut command rather the Copy command.

1. Select the file(s) or folder(s) that you would like to move.

2. Right-click the selection you would like to move. A menu will appear.

3. Click Cut. The icon(s) of the selection will appear dimmed.

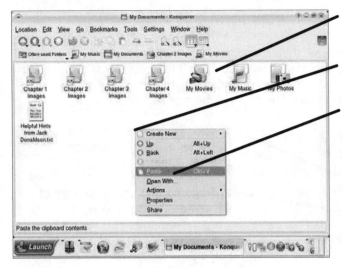

4.  Navigate to the location where you would like to move the file.

5.  Right-click in any blank area of the screen. A menu will appear.

6.  Click Paste. The selection will be moved to this location. Alternatively you can click the Paste button that is located on the toolbar.

## Renaming Files

Whether you want to give your files and directories more specific names or you just don't like the name you originally selected, you can quickly change their names.

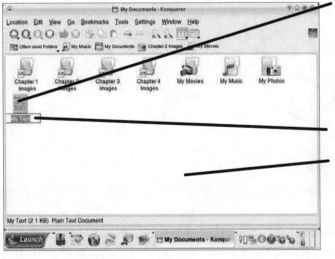

1.  Click a file or folder that you would like to rename. It will be highlighted.

2.  Press the F2 key on your keyboard. The name of the file will now be highlighted and you can give it a new name.

3.  Type a new name for your file.

4.  Press Enter on the keyboard or click anywhere else on the screen. Your file will now have a new name.

## Creating Folders

Folders are an essential part of keeping the files on your computer organized. While Linspire provides some folders for you to start with, such as "My Documents," it is a good idea to create additional folders to further organize and categorize your work. The process of creating a folder involves just a few clicks of the mouse button.

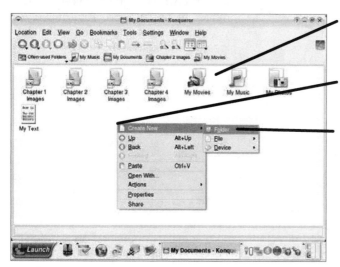

1. Navigate to the location on your computer where you would like to create a folder.

2. Right-click in any blank area of the screen. A menu will appear.

3. Click Create New and then click Folder... A dialog box will appear asking you to name your new folder.

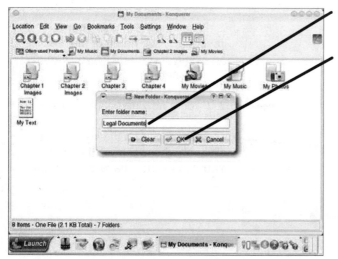

4. Type a name for your folder that best describes its contents.

5. Click OK. The folder will be created.

## Getting File Information

There are literally thousands of different types of files that your Linspire computer can store. Using the Detailed List View is one method for getting some information about your file, but there is a much faster method.

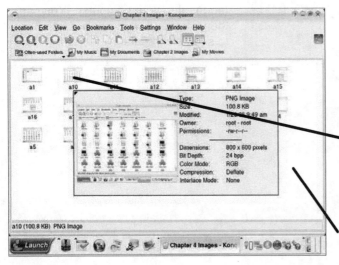

1. Hover your mouse pointer over any icon in the File Manager. After a second or two a little window will open with a variety of information on your file.

2. Move your mouse pointer away from the icon and the window will close.

## Viewing Files from CD-ROMS and Other Drives

The quickest way to view the contents of files on a CD or floppy drive is to use the icons on your desktop. By double-clicking the CD or Floppy icon, the File Manager will open with the contents of those devices in view. You can also view the contents of any mounted drive from the File Manager by navigating to the "mnt" folder.

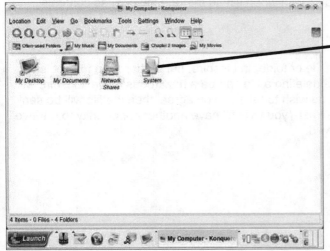

1. Double-click the System folder icon. The screen will change to show you the contents of the folder.

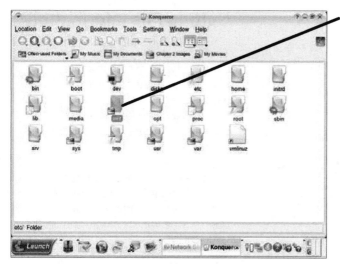

2. Double-click the "mnt" folder. You will now see all of the drives that are mounted to your computer. You can then double-click the desired device to see its contents.

# The Trash

Unlike with regular trash, in Linspire you don't have to drag yourself out of bed early in the morning, endure the cold weather and carry heavy bags to your curb when you want to get rid of a file or folder. The trash folder itself is your safety net. When you delete a file in Linspire, the file is sent to the trash folder instead of it being erased entirely. Think of the trash as a dumpster at the back of a building. If you inadvertently throw something out, you can rummage through the dumpster to retrieve it. Don't worry, Linspire does not have any rats or banana peels to deal with when sifting through the deleted contents.

## Deleting Items

There are several ways to delete a file or folder in Linspire, but perhaps the fastest is to simply use the keyboard. Because deleting a file can be a hazardous move, Linspire will first confirm that this is the action you wish to take. If you agree, then the file will be sent to the trash folder. Once it's in the trash, you will still have another opportunity to retrieve the file if it was inadvertently removed.

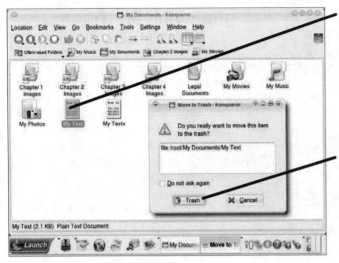

1. Select the file or folder or icon that you wish to delete. The selected file will be highlighted.

2. Press the Delete key on your keyboard. A dialog box will appear confirming that you want to send this item to the trash folder.

3. Click the Trash button. The file will be sent to the trash folder.

*You can bypass the Trash and completely delete a file by holding down the Shift key as you press Delete. A dialog box will appear confirming that your want to delete the file.*

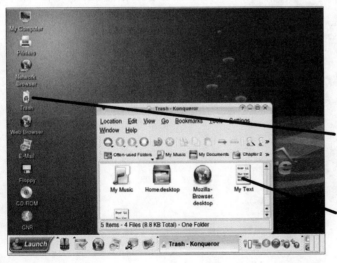

## Viewing and Reclaiming Trashed Items

If you've trashed an item inadvertently or if you now realize that you actually need an item that you have trashed, it can be retrieved.

1. Double-click the Trash icon on your desktop. The File Manager will open to the folder that contains the trash.

2. Cut and paste your file to any other location.

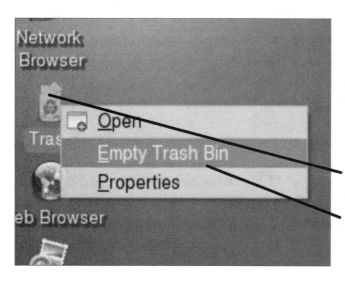

## Emptying the Trash

If you no longer require the files that you have sent to the Trash, you can empty the files in the Trash folder. Keep in mind though that once the Trash has been emptied, the files are gone for good.

1. Right-click the Trash icon. A menu will appear.

2. Click Empty Trash Bin. The files in the Trash Bin will be permanently deleted.

# Finding Files

While having a good filing system goes a long way to keeping you organized, there will often be times when you just can't seem to find a file you're looking for when navigating the File Manager. For these occasions you can take advantage of Linspire's search functionality.

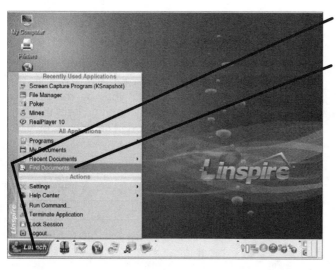

1. Click the Launch button. The Launch menu will appear.

2. Click Find Documents. The Find Files dialog box will open and you can begin the search process.

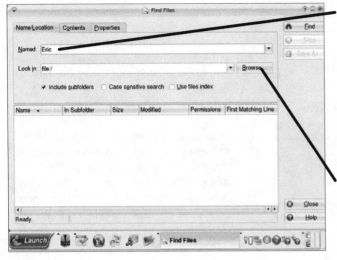

3.  In the Named: box type a name for the file that you want to retrieve. If you don't know the name of the file, but only know what type of file it is, you can put a * in the Named: field, followed by the file type.  For example, if you wanted to find all of the mp3 files in a particular location you would type *.mp3 in the Named: field.

4.  Click the Browse button.  You can now select where you want to conduct the search.

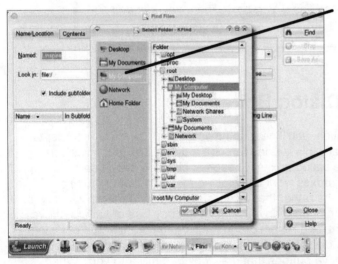

5.  Click My Computer if you want to search your entire computer for the file.  Otherwise, if you only want to search in a particular folder, you can click the folder from right side of the dialog box.  Double-click to expand a folder to see if there are any subfolders within.

6.  Click OK.  You will return to the Find Files dialog box.

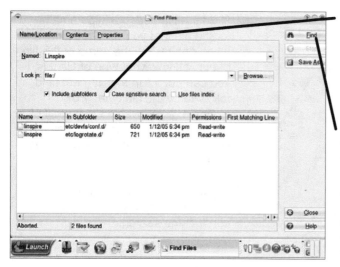

7. Click any of the check boxes to select or deselect any other search criteria. This includes looking in subfolders, conducting a case sensitive search and using the files index.

8. Click Find. All the files that match your search criteria will be listed in the window. Included in the search results will be the location of the file along with other file details. You can now conduct another search or close down the window by clicking the Close button in the top right corner of the window.

*You can conduct more detailed searches by clicking on the Contents or Properties tab in the Find Files dialog box. There you can add additional criteria to your search.*

# File Management with Dialog Boxes

In almost every computer application, you'll need to navigate your computer in order to select, open, or save files. Typically this is done through a dialog box that gives you access to your files. Although the dialog boxes for each application are different, in many cases the way in which the dialog boxes work is almost identical to that of the File Manager. You can use dialog boxes rather than accessing the File Manager whenever you want to navigate your computer's hard drive, select and copy files or folders, move files, or even create folders. Because different programs have different styles of dialog boxes, you'll have to examine the dialog boxes closely to see what features they offer. Some of these dialog boxes will have buttons that may look unfamiliar to you. When dealing with unfamiliar buttons in a dialog box, the best idea is to hover your mouse pointer over the button. In most cases, after a second or two, a tool tip will appear that will describe the function of the button. Another good idea is to right-click a file in a dialog box to see what options are available. On the next page you'll find examples of dialog boxes from different programs that offer some file management capabilities.

## Dialog Box Example One

This is the Open dialog box from OpenOffice Word Processor.  As you can see there are various File Management functions available.

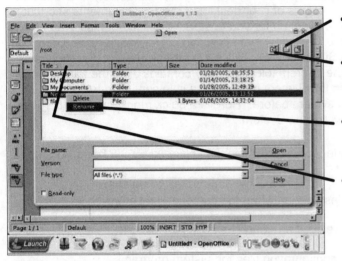

- New Folder.  Lets you create a new folder to store files.

- Up.  This feature will allow you to move up one level in file hierarchy.

- Right-Click Menu.  Right-clicking on a file in this dialog box lets you rename or delete files.

- Sort.  You can sort files by clicking on the column heading.

## Dialog Box Example Two

This is the Open dialog box from the Image Viewer.  As you can see there are various file management functions that look quite different from the File Manager.

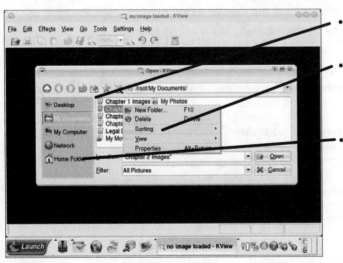

- New Folder.  Lets you create a new folder to store files.

- Right-Click Menu.  When you right-click on a file in this dialog box you can sort your files or view their properties.

- Navigation Buttons.  This dialog box has various navigation buttons that allow you to quickly jump to certain areas.

# Understanding Linspire Folders

When you first start the File Manager, you are taken to the Home window, which includes four icons that are pretty self explanatory. The My Desktop shortcut takes you to a folder on your system that contains the contents of your desktop. The My Documents shortcut takes you to a folder that Linspire has set up for you to store your documents. The Network Shares shortcut takes you to window that allows you to view other computers on your network. Finally there is the System folder. While the other icons are just shortcuts to folders within your computer, the System folder actually contains all of the folders on your computer. The folders within the System may seem a little confusing to you if you haven't worked on a Linux-based system before. Here is a quick rundown of the purpose of most of the folders contained within the System:

- bin. Short for binary, the bin folder contains the binary files need for the key programs and operating system to run.

- boot. This folder contains the files needed when the computer first starts.

- dev. The files that control your devices are found here.

- etc. This folder contains critical configuration files for system programs.

- home. This is the folder that each user logs into at the start of a session.

- lib. This folder contains the libraries that are used by the programs on your system.

*Do not delete any of the folders found directly within the System folder. Many of the files contained within these folders are essential for your programs and operating system to run.*

- mnt. This folder contains your mounted hardware like different floppys or CD drives.

- opt. This folder contains information on add-on programs.

- proc. This folder contains information that is stored in the computer's memory.

- root. This contains the files of the administrator account.

- sbin.  This folder contains the binary files used for administering system functions.

- tmp.  This folder contains temporary files.

- usr.  The application files for the software you've installed are found in this directory.

- var.  This folder contains files that vary in size while the system is operating.

*Unlike the File Manager, the dialog boxes in some of your programs may not give you direct access to you're my Documents folder.  It can usually be found in  /root/My Computer.*

# Archiving Files

When I was fourteen, I got my first job at McDonald's and one of my responsibilities was to take the garbage to the back and put it through the compacter.  I was always so amazed at how much garbage could fit in the dumpster after it had been compacted.  Your Linspire computer has a compactor built in.  If you're finding that you're getting low on hard drive space you can archive some files.  Archiving basically compacts the files so that they don't take up as much space.  Archiving is also particularly useful when sending e-mails.  If you have a file that is too large to send over e-mail, you can archive it to reduce its file size.  Within Linspire there is a program called the Archiving & Zip Tool that will not only allow you to archive files, but you can also expand archived files that have been sent to you.  You can select from a variety of different compression formats to archive you files.

1. Click Launch | Run Programs. A list of program categories will appear.

2. Click Utilities. A variety of utility programs will appear.

3. Click Archiving & Zip Tool. The Archiving & Zip program will open.

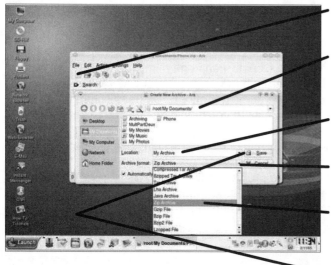

4. Click the New button. The Create New Archive dialog box will open.

5. Navigate to the location where you would like your archive to be created.

6. Type a name for your archive in the Location field.

7. Click the drop-down menu to see a list of archive compression types.

8. Click the desired method. If you are unclear of which one to select, choose zip.

9. Click the Save button.

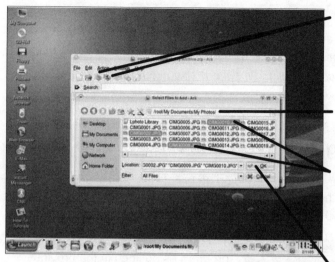

10. Click the Add File or the Add Folder buttons. A dialog box will appear where you can select the files or folders that you would like to add to your archive.

11. Navigate to the folder that contains the file that you would like to archive.

12. Click on the desired file. It will be highlighted. You can hold down the Ctrl key and click on any other files in that folder that you would like to add to the archive.

13. Click OK. The files you selected will now be added to the archive.

*The amount that a file will compressed will depend on two factors: the type of compression method you have selected (zip, tar, etc.) and the original file type.*

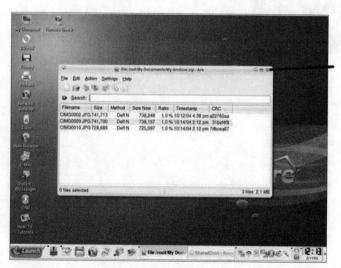

14. Repeat Steps 8 - 12 to add any other files or folders to your archive.

15. Click the Close button to shut down the Archiving & Zip Tool program. All the files within the archive will now be compressed.

*Many e-mail programs will block messages that contain an attachment that has been archived using the zip method. You may want to use a different compression type if e-mailing your files.*

# Unzipping or Expanding Archived Files

Unzipping has become the popular term for expanding archived files, and is used universally regardless of whether the archive is a zip file or not. The actually process of expanding an archive is quite straightforward.

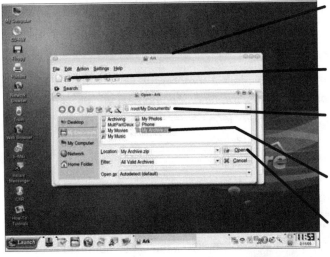

1. Open the Archiving & Zip Tool program as outlined in the previous section.

2. Click the Open button. The Open dialog box will appear.

3. Navigate to the folder that contains the archived file you'd like to expand.

4. Click on the archive that you would like to expand.

5. Click Open. The archive will open and you will be able to view its contents.

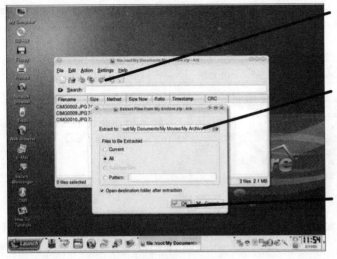

6. Click the Extract button. A dialog box will open where you can specify the location for the folder to be extracted.

7. Type the location of where you would like the folder extracted. Alternatively, you can click the little blue folder to the right of the browse field to bring open a dialog box where you can select a folder.

8. Click the OK button. The files will be extracted to the location you specified. The folder where you extracted the files will also open.

# Burning Files to CD

With the low price of both CD burners and CDRs (writeable CDs) many people are sharing and storing files by burning them to CD. Whether you want to share your favorite photos with friends or simply back up your files, Linspire makes it a breeze. There are actually several ways to burn a CD, here we'll explore using the CD & DVD Burning program.

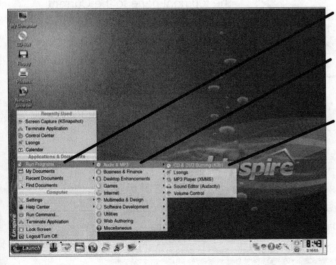

1. Click Launch | Run Programs. A submenu of categories will appear.

2. Click Audio & MP3. A variety of programs under that category will appear.

3. Click CD & DVD Burning. This will launch a program that will allow you to burn files to CD. The first time you launch the program, you will be asked to enter the write speed of your CD burner. This information should be available from the company you purchased your computer or CD burner from.

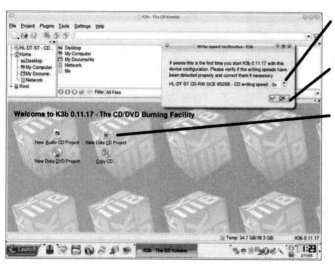

4. Use the arrow keys to enter the write speed of your CD writer.

5. Click OK. The dialog box will close.

6. Click New Data CD Project. You will now be able to select files and/or folders to include on your CD.

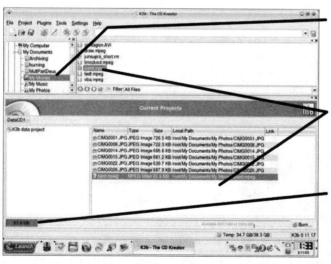

7. Double-click a folder in the left pane of the window to reveal its contents. You can browse through different folders just as you would in the File Manager.

8. Click and drag a file or folder from the top right pane to the Current Projects window. The file will be added to the CD project.

9. Review the green bar that indicates how large your project is.

10. Repeat Steps 7 - 9 until you have completed adding data to your project.

*Most CDs allow you to add up to 700MB of files. If you are burning your files to a DVD you can typically store up to 4.7 GB of data.*

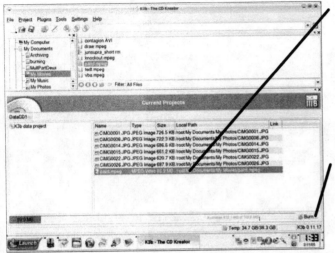

11.  Click on any file that you would like to remove from your project.

12.  Click the Delete key on your keyboard.  The file will be removed from the project.

13.  Insert a writeable CD into your CD burner.

14.  Click Burn.  A dialog box will appear where you can adjust settings for your burner.

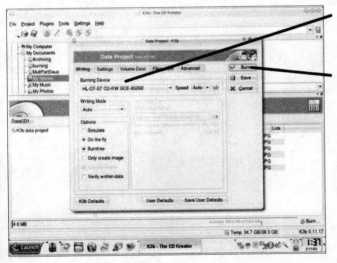

15.  Review the settings and make any changes if desired.  Typically you can just leave these settings as is.

16.  Click the Burn button.  The process of copying the files to CD will begin.  A progress indicator will appear on the screen letting you know what percentage of the project is complete.  When it is finished, the CD will be ejected from the CD drive and a trumpet sound will play indicating that everything went successfully.

# Word Processing

**5**

Typically when you purchase a computer, you are given only a bare bones system with little useful software. In order to do anything meaningful with it, you must go out and spend money on a suite of software - typically an office suite with a word processor, a spreadsheet and a slide show program.

Your Linspire computer comes pre-installed with the OpenOffice suite. This office suite is not your run-of-the-mill, freebie software package. It is jam-packed with features to meet all your document, spreadsheet and slide show needs. If you're migrating from Microsoft Windows to Linspire, you'll find making the switch to OpenOffice a breeze. The functionality is almost identical and the document conversion is almost flawless. Word Processor is the cornerstone of the OpenOffice suite. It provides you with all of the components you'll need to create just about any type of document  Although it would take an entire book to cover all of the features of Word Processor, the goal of this chapter is to give you a thorough grounding in the program and take you beyond just the basics of creating documents.

In this chapter we'll cover:

- Document file basics

- Page setup

- Basic and advanced formatting

# Launching Word Processor

The entire OpenOffice suite is located in the Business & Finance section of the Launch menu. All of the programs, including Word Processor, Spreadsheets, Drawings and Presentations can be found there.

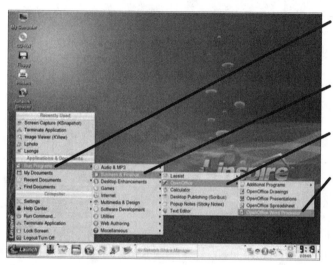

1. Click the Launch button then click Run Programs. A list of categories will appear.

3. Click Business & Finance. A submenu will appear.

4. Click OpenOffice. Another submenu will appear.

5. Click OpenOffice Word Processor. This action will launch the Word Processor.

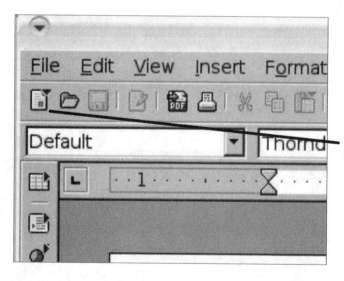

# Creating a New Document

If you're interested in creating a document from scratch, you can do so easily.

1. Click the New button on the toolbar. A blank document will open.

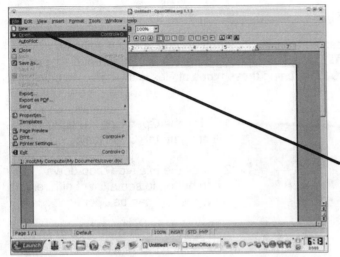

# Opening an Existing Document

There will be many occasions when you will want to continue working on a document that you have previously been working on. In these cases, you simply have to open the file.

1. Click File | Open. The Open dialog box will appear.

*The keyboard shortcut to execute the Open command is Ctrl+O.*

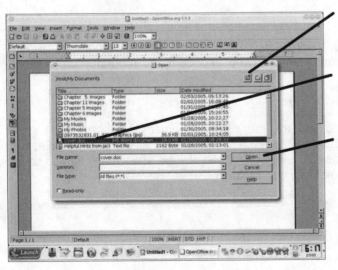

2. Navigate to the folder that contains the file that you would like to open.

3. Click the desired file that you would like to open. The file will be highlighted.

4. Click Open. The file that you have selected will open.

# Opening Other Formats

Believe it or not, not everyone creates all their documents using the same software program. No worries though, Word Processor supports a multitude of different file types that you can open. The procedure for opening these types of files is the same as any other file.

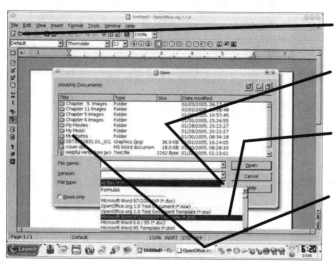

1. Click the Open icon. This action will bring up the Open dialog box.

2. Click the File type drop-down menu button to see a list of different file types that can be opened.

3. Click the desired file type to see only those types of files in the dialog box.

4. Click the desired file that you would like to open and press Enter on the keyboard. The file that you have selected will open.

# Saving

Everyone has a horror story about losing some or all of their work due to computer failure, power outage, etc. It's always a good idea to save your documents frequently.

## Save As...

The Save As function allows you to save and name your document at the same time. The first time you save a new document, the Save As dialog box will appear, regardless of whether you choose Save or Save As... Save As can also be used at any time to save your document under a new name or in a new location.

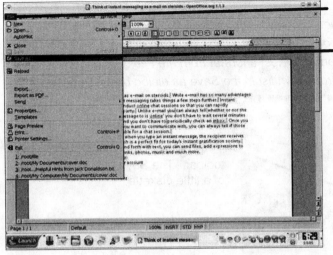

1. Click File. The File menu will
expand.

2. Click Save As… The Save As
dialog box will open.

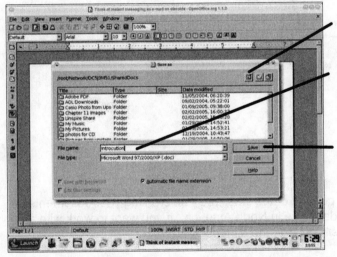

3. Navigate to the folder where you
want to save your file.

4. Type a name for your document.
It's a good idea to give it a name that
best describes the contents of your
document.

5. Click Save. The file will be saved
with the name you gave it in the
selected folder.

# Save

After you've saved your file for the first time you should save it occasionally as you work
in your document and when you have finished your edits.

*When you save a document, it is saved in its original file format. To save it to a different format, select a format from the File type drop-down list in the Save as dialog box.*

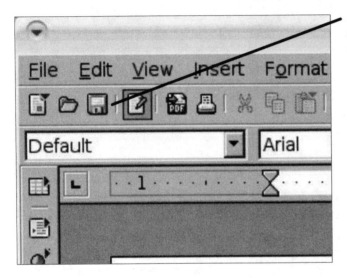

1. Click the Save button in the toolbar. The Save button is an icon of a little diskette.

## Page Size and Margins

The truth of the matter is that 99 percent of the time, you'll be creating your documents on 8.5 x 11 paper, which is the standard size in North America. If you want to work with a different size of paper, you to easily change the dimensions.

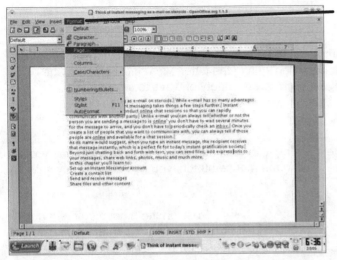

1.  Click Format.  The Format menu will appear.

2.  Click Page.   The Page Style dialog box will open.  You will now have options for the page setup.

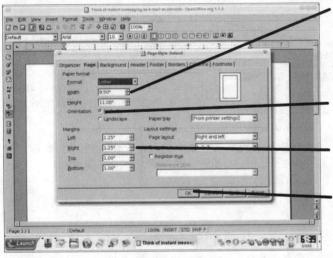

3.  Click the arrow keys to adjust the width and height of the page. Alternatively you can select preset sizes from the Format drop-down menu.

4.  Click the radio button beside the desired page orientation.

5.  Click the arrow keys to adjust the page margins.

6.  Click OK. The changes you applied will take effect.

# Selecting Text

Before you can format text, you first must tell Word Processor what text you would like to format. You can perform this action by highlighting the letter, word, paragraph, page or pages that you would like to change. There are a variety of ways to select text.

## Selecting with the Mouse

The most common way to select text is simply to click and drag across the text that you would like to select with the mouse. Using the mouse button, you can also quickly select different ranges.

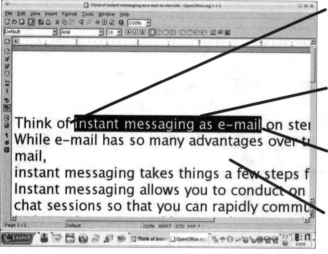

1.  Position the mouse pointer right before the word, sentence or paragraph that you would like to select.

2.  Click and drag to the right. As you drag the words that the cursor passes over will be selected.

3.  Release the mouse button. The area that you highlighted will now be selected.

4.  Click in any blank area of the document to deselect the text.

*If you double-click a word, the entire word will be selected. If you triple-click a word, the entire line will be selected. If you press Ctrl+A, everything in your document will be selected.*

## Selecting with the Keyboard

To select text, you can also use the keyboard in conjunction with the mouse.

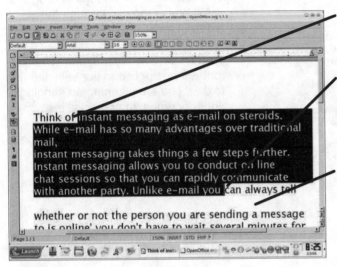

1. Click a location where you want a selection to begin. The cursor will flash in that location.

2. Hold down the Shift key and click where you would like the selection to end. A selection will be created from the point you clicked in Step 1 to where you have now clicked.

3. Click in any other location to deselect your selection.

# Fonts

Imagine going into McDonald's and only being able to order a hamburger. No cheeseburgers, no Big Macs, no fries, no shakes, just hamburgers. I'm sure you and millions of others wouldn't be very happy; we all like choice. Everybody has different tastes, and tastes in fonts are no different. For this reason, Word Processor allows you to select from any fonts that you have installed on your system.

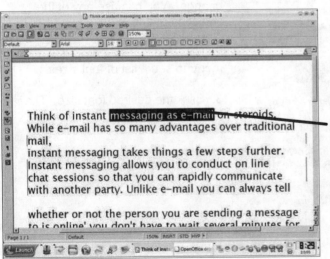

1. Create a selection that contains the text that you want to change. You can use any of the selection methods. If you don't make a selection before you change any aspect of a font, the changes will take effect on any new text that you type from the point of your cursor onwards.

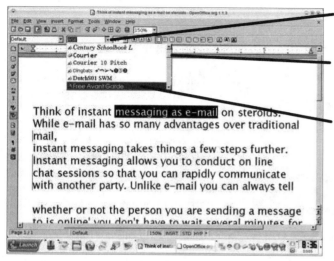

2. Click on the font drop-down menu to see a list of fonts.

3. Click the scroll buttons or drag the scroll box to browse through the different fonts.

4. Click on the desired font. The font will be applied to the selected text. If you are planning on sending your document to someone else, to view on their computer, they must have the same font, otherwise a font substitution will be made.

## Font Size

When you change the size of a font, you not only change its height and width, you also change the amount of space between the lines of text.

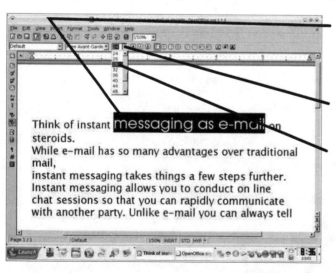

1. Create a selection that contains the text whose size you want to change. You can use any of the selection methods.

2. Click the font size drop-down menu to see a list of font sizes.

3. Click the desired font size. The size will be applied to the selected text.

# Font Color

Using color you can make certain elements of your document stand out from others. Keep in mind that certain colors may make your document difficult to read.

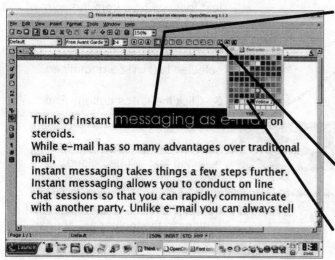

1. Create a selection that contains the text that you want to change. You can use any of the selection methods. If you don't make a selection before you change any aspect of a font, the changes will take effect on any new text that you type from the point of your cursor onwards.

2. Click and hold the Font Color button. A palette of colors will appear.

3. Click the desired color. The color of the selected text will change. You can click the Close button in the Font color window to close it.

# Bold, Italics and Underline

I remember it was the early '80s when I first worked on a computer. I was so excited by its ability to bold, italicize, and underline text. While these three effects have been used and abused throughout the years, they still prove to be valuable.

*The keyboard shortcuts for the Bold, Italics and Underline commands are Ctrl+B, Ctrl+I and Ctrl+U respectively.*

1. Create a selection that contains the text you want to change. If you don't make a selection before you change any aspect of a font, the changes will take effect on any new text that you type from the point of your cursor onwards.

2. Click the Underline button. The selected text will be underlined.

3. Click the Italics button. The selected text will be italicized.

4. Click the Bold button. The selected text will be bolded.

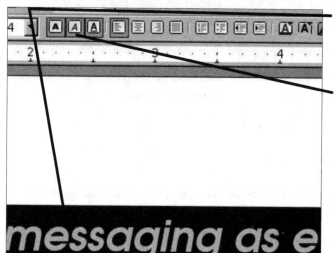

5. Select any text that has been bolded, italicized or underlined. The buttons in the toolbar will appear highlighted.

6. Click on any of the buttons to remove that effect for the selected text.

## Other Font Effects

In addition to the traditional effects, there are a variety of other font effects that you can apply. These effects include things like adding custom underlines, embossing text, adding shadows and making text blink.

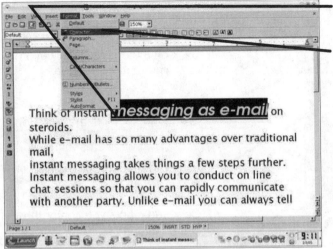

1. Create a selection that contains the text you want to change.

2. Click Format | Character... A dialog box will appear where you can add different effects.

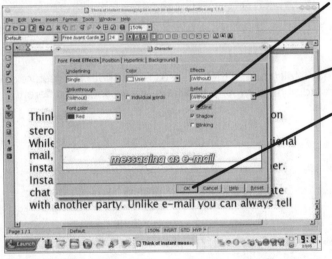

3. Click the check box beside the different effects that you would like to apply.

4. Click any of the drop-down menus to select from different effects.

5. Click OK. The effect will be applied to the selected text.

# Justification

Changing how your text is justified is a breeze. Simply select the text and then choose the desired justification method.

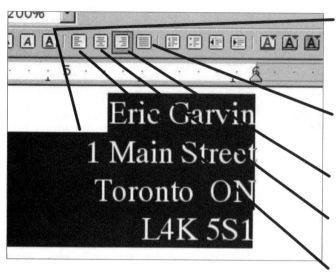

1. Create a selection that contains the text you want to justify.

2. Click on the desired justification button. Your options include:

- Justified – Lets you spread the text to the edges of the page for any full lines.

- Align Right - Lets you align all of the text to the right side.

- Centered – Lets you center the text on the page.

- Align Left - Lets you align all of the text to the left side.

# Numbering

Ask many legal secretaries and they'll tell you that they couldn't live without this feature. Being able to number lines and paragraphs is important. There are a variety of different ways you can create numbered lists.

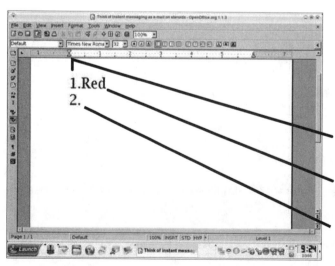

## Auto-Numbered Lists

By default, the auto-numbered lists feature is turned on. This feature allows you to create a numbered list automatically simply by using the tab key.

1. Type the number 1 and a period and then press the Tab key.

2. Type in the text that you would like as your first line.

3. Press the Enter key. The number 2. will automatically appear.

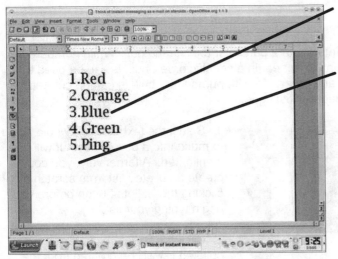

4.  Repeat Steps 2 - 3 for any remaining items that you would like to add to your numbered list.

5.  Press the Enter key twice to end the numbered list.

## Numbering Button

If you have an existing body of text, you can create a numbered list from it using the Numbering button.  Wherever there is a hard return in your text, a new number will be created for your list.  Alternatively you can start by pressing the Number button to create your numbered list from scratch.

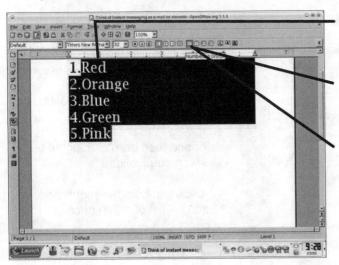

1.  Select the text that you would like to make into a numbered list.  It will be highlighted.

2.  Click the Numbering button.  A numbered list will be created from the selected text.

3.  Click the Numbering button again to remove the numbered list.

# Bullets

Bullets are used to make key points about a particular topic stand out.  While numbered lists are used when information has to appear in a specific order, bullets can be used to emphasize lists of information in any order.  As with numbering, bullets can be created from scratch or they can be applied to existing text.

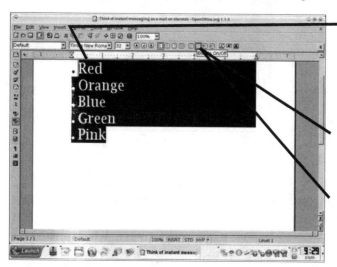

1.  Select the text that you would like to make into a bulleted list.  It will be highlighted.  Alternatively, you could create a bulleted list from scratch by clicking the Bullets button before you begin typing your list.

2.  Click the Bullets button.  A bulleted list will be created from the selected text.

3.  Click the Bullets button again to remove the numbered list.

# Highlighting

When you were making notes from your textbooks in school, you probably highlighted certain passages so that you could quickly reference them later.  Word Processor has a Highlight tool that mimics real-life highlighting.  You simply have to select a highlighter color and then drag across the text you want to highlight.

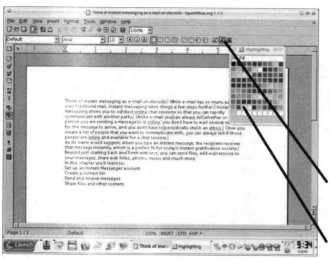

1.  Click and hold the Highlight button.  A list of different colors will appear.

2.  Click the desired highlighter color.

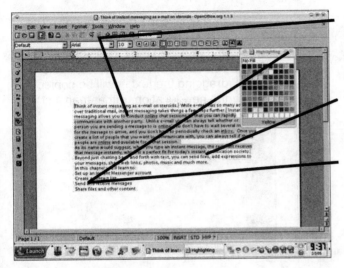

3. Click and drag, across the text that you would like to highlight. As you drag it will appear like it is being selected.

4. Release the mouse button. The text that you dragged over will be highlighted.

5. Click the "X" in the top right corner of the Highlighting window to close it when you are finished.

*To remove highlighting, follow the same steps above with one exception. In Step 2, select the No Fill option in the Highlighting window where you select a color.*

## Moving Text

It's common to have to move a block of text to another location in your document. This can be done very quickly by simply clicking and dragging.

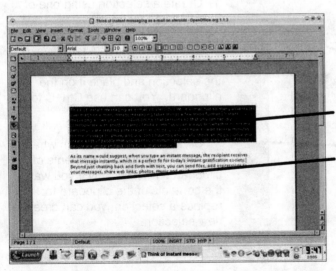

1. Create a selection of text using one of the selection methods.

2. Click and drag the selection to the desired location. As you drag, your mouse pointer will have a little square attached to it. A cursor will appear indicating where the text will be moved.

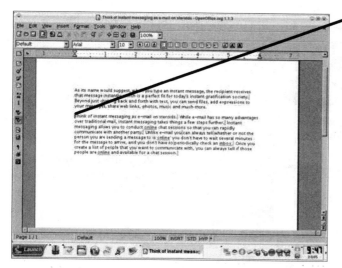

3. Release the mouse button.  The text will be moved to the point where you released the mouse button.  If you hold down the Ctrl key while dragging the text, it will be copied to the new location, rather than just moved.

# Cutting, Copying, and Pasting

Cutting, copying and pasting are the backbone of document editing in Word Processor.  When you cut or copy objects, they are placed on a virtual clipboard that stores the items so that it can be pasted elsewhere.  Cutting removes the object from the document to be placed on the clipboard, while copying makes a duplicate of your object on the clipboard.

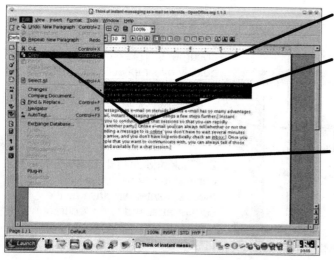

1. Create a selection using one of the selection methods.

2. Click Edit | Copy.  Alternatively you can select Edit | Cut to remove the selection and place it on the clipboard.  You can use Ctrl+C to copy or Ctrl+X to paste.

3. Click once at the location where you want to place the contents of the clipboard.  Alternatively if you want the contents of the clipboard to replace a selection, you can create a new selection.

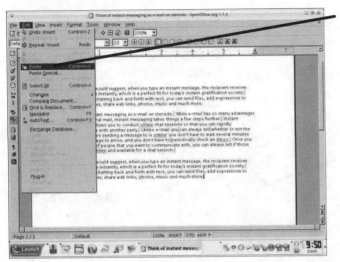

4.  Click Edit | Paste.  The contents of the clipboard will be placed at the point you selected in Step 3.

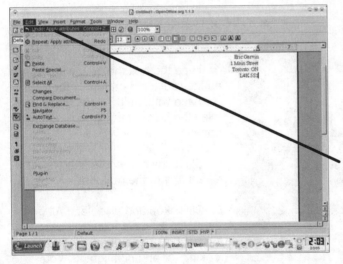

# Undoing

What's a pencil without an eraser? Everyone makes mistakes and Word Processor doesn't expect you to be any different.  If you make an error, you can use the undo feature to go back a step.

1.  Click Edit | Undo.  The last action that you took will be undone.

2.  Repeat Step 1 until you have returned to the desired point in your document.

*Ctrl+Z is the universal shortcut for the Undo command.  Not only will it work in Word Processor, it will work in many other applications.*

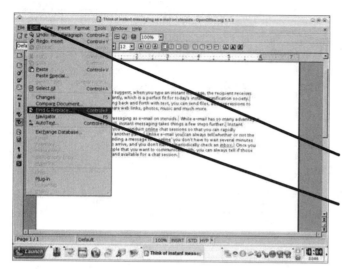

# Find and Replace

The Find and Replace feature allows you to search through your document, find a particular item and then, if you'd like, replace it with something else.

1. Click Edit.  The Edit menu appears.

2.  Click Find & Replace...  The Find and Replace dialog will open.

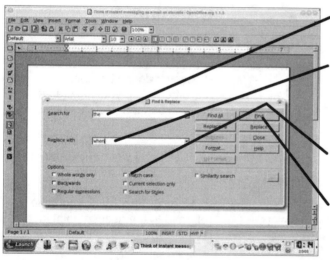

3. Type the text that you are looking for in the Search for: field.

4.  Type the text that you want to use as the replacement text in the Replace with: field.  You can skip this step if you are just looking for a particular word or words.

5.  Click any of the check boxes to select any of the options.

6.  Click Replace,  Replace All or Find.  Clicking Replace will jump to the next instance of the text you are looking for and highlight it.  You must click Replace again to actually replace the text.  Clicking Replace All will replace all the instances.  Clicking Find will find the next instance of the word.  You will need to continue pressing Find to move to the next instance of the text.

# Creating Spreadsheets

Spreadsheet is a powerful software application that allows you to store, manipulate and display data in a variety of formats. The uses for spreadsheets are limited only by your imagination. Everything from business financials, stock portfolios, baseball statistics, invitation lists, invoices and much, much more can be stored in spreadsheets.

At first glance, a spreadsheet can look intimidated with its seemingly endless grid of rows and columns. The truth is that once you understand the basics of creating and working within spreadsheets, you'll get addicted quickly. Because Spreadsheet is part of the OpenOffice suite, many of the basic functionality is the same as the other components of the suite. For that reason, you can refer back to Chapter 5: "Word Processing" if you need a refresher on some of the file basics including opening, saving and creating new documents.

In this chapter we'll cover:

- Entering data into a spreadsheet
- Using formulas
- Formatting worksheets
- Creating charts

6

# Launching Spreadsheet

The entire OpenOffice suite is located in the Business & Finance section of the Launch Menu. All of the programs, including Word Processor, Spreadsheet, Drawings and Presentations can be found there.

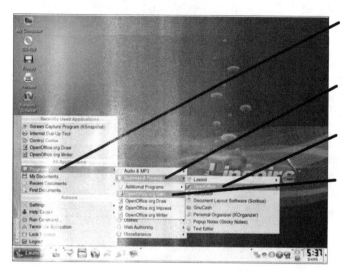

1. Click the Launch button and then click Run Programs. A list of categories will appear.

2. Click Business & Finance. A submenu will appear.

3. Click OpenOffice. Another submenu will appear.

4. Click OpenOffice Spreadsheet to launch the Spreadsheet program.

# Entering Data

Once you have a spreadsheet open, you can begin entering data. Typically, data in a spreadsheet takes on one of three forms, either text (sometimes this is referred to as a "label"), numbers or formulas. The distinction between the three forms is how you enter them.

## Entering Formulas

To be considered a formula, the data that you enter must begin with an operator. The equals sign (=) is the operator that lets Spreadsheet know you are entering a formula. Formulas will be covered later in the chapter, but for now, it's just important to note that an operator is needed to start a formula.

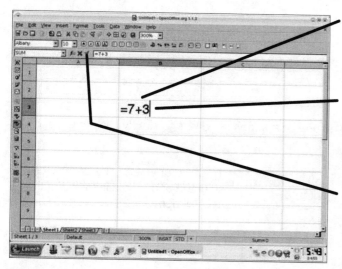

1. Click once in the cell that you would like to add a formula to. It will be highlighted to indicate that it is selected.

2. Type the equals sign (=) followed by the mathematical formula. The equals sign will appear in the cell and in the formula bar. Formulas are covered in detail later in the chapter.

3. Click the check mark in the formula bar when you are finished entering your formula or simply press the Enter key on the keyboard. The results of the formula will appear in the cell.

## Entering Text and Values

Entering text and numbers into your cells is simply a matter of typing. Once you've selected the cell that you want to enter text into, the rest is a breeze.

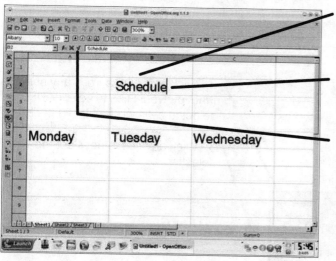

1. Click the cell into which you would like to add text or numbers. The cell will be highlighted

2. Type your text. Ensure that it does not start with an equals (=) sign.

3. Click the check mark in the formula bar when you are finished entering your formula or press Enter on the keyboard.

# Making Selections

Before you can format, edit, or manipulate a cell or cells they must first be selected.

## Clicking and Dragging

Probably the quickest way to select one or a series of cells is to simply click and drag across them.

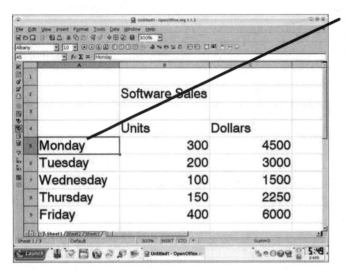

1. Click any cell. The cell will be selected and an outline around the cell will appear.

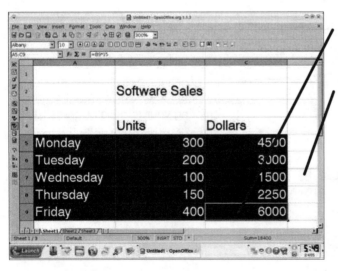

2. Click and drag across any cells that you would like to select. The selected cells will be highlighted.

3. Click any cell to deselect the selection.

## Selecting Entire Rows or Columns

At the top of every column and to the left of every row there is a letter or a number called the column or row heading. By clicking on these row or column headings you can select entire rows or columns.

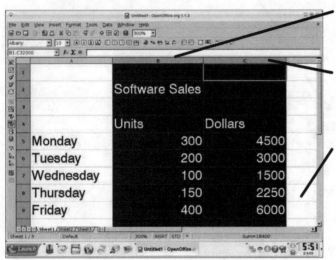

1. Click a row or column heading. The entire row or column will be selected.

2. Click and drag across row or column headings. As you drag multiple rows and columns will be selected.

3. Click any individual cell. This action will deselect your selection.

*Pressing Ctrl+A on your keyboard will select all of the cells in your spreadsheet. Holding down the Ctrl key as you click cells lets you select cells that aren't together.*

# Worksheets

The files that you create in Spreadsheet are called workbooks. Within each workbook there are a series of worksheets where you can enter your data. These sheets are perfect for breaking up data into logical categories so your spreadsheet doesn't become too confusing. By default, three worksheets are created in every new workbook. Spreadsheet allows you to create additional worksheets, name them, and organize them.

## Accessing Sheets

To access a worksheet you have to click the tab associated with it.

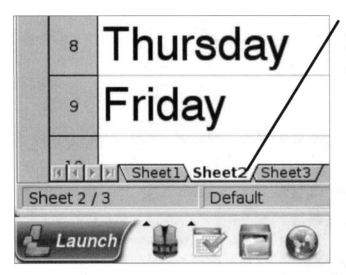

1. Click on the tab associated with the worksheet you want to open. The worksheet will now become active.

## Creating Sheets

If you require more than the three worksheets that are created with every workbook, you can easily create and configure new ones from the Insert Sheet dialog box.

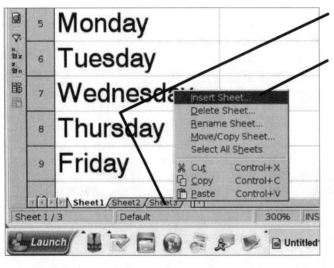

1. Right-click on any tab. A menu will appear.

2. Click Insert Sheet... The Insert Sheet dialog box will open.

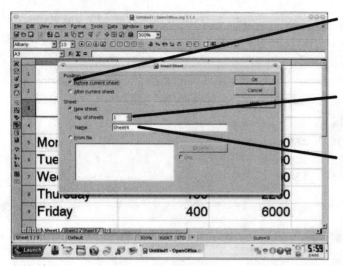

3.  Click the radio button beside the desired location for the new sheet, either before or after the current sheet.

4.  Click the up arrow key to increase the number of sheets you'd like to add.

5.  Type a name for your sheet if desired.

6.  Press Enter or click the OK button.  The new  sheet will be added to your workbook.

*To change the order that worksheets appear, position your mouse pointer over the tab of the worksheet you want to move, and click and drag it before or after other tabs.*

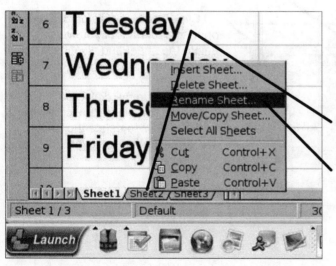

## Naming Worksheets

The names Sheet 1, Sheet 2, Sheet 3, etc. aren't the most descriptive of names.  You can rename the sheet tabs to something more appropriate.

1.  Right-click on the tab of any worksheet you would like to rename.

2.  Click Rename Sheet...  A dialog box will open where you can rename your sheet.

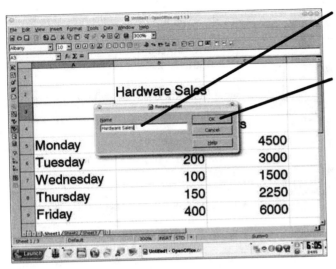

3. Type a new name for the sheet. It's a good idea to give the sheet a descriptive name.

4. Press the OK button. The sheet will now be renamed.

# Deleting Sheets

You can remove any sheet from your workbook. Just be careful when you delete a sheet as you will lose all the data on that sheet.

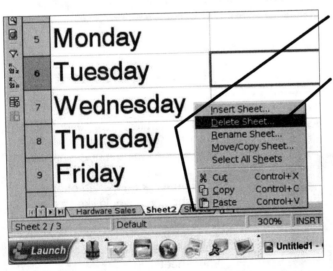

1. Right-click the tab of the sheet that you would like to remove. A menu will now appear.

2. Click Delete. A dialog box will open to confirm that you want to delete the sheet and all of its contents.

3. Click OK in the dialog box that appears. The dialog box confirms that you want to delete the sheet. The sheet will be removed.

# Adding or Deleting Rows and Columns

Once you have entered data, you may find it necessary to add a row or a column to your sheet.  You have the ability to add or delete single or multiple rows at any time.

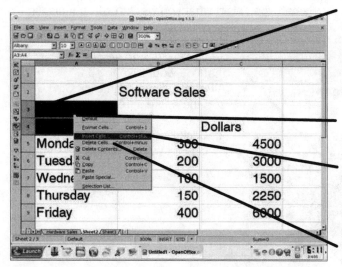

1.  Click a cell or create a selection where you would like to add or delete a row or column.  The number of cells you select will indicate how many rows or columns will be added or deleted.

2.  Right-click anywhere on your selection.  A menu will appear.

3.  Click Insert Cells...  The Insert dialog box will appear.

Or

3.  Click Delete Cells... This will delete the selected rows or columns.

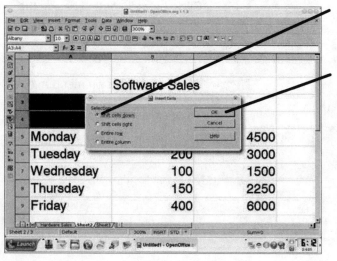

4.  Click the radio beside the selected option for inserting or deleting rows or columns.

5.  Click OK.  The dialog box will close and rows or columns will be added or removed based on the settings you have entered.

# Sorting Data

Remember in primary school when your class would have to line up from shortest to tallest? Aside from denigrating the really short or the really tall, it gave you a valuable lesson in sorting. Sorting, in essence, changes the order of how your information is displayed in the spreadsheet. Not only can you select what you want to sort but also in what order it appears.

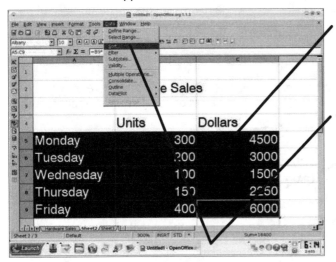

1. Click and drag across the data that you would like to sort. Alternatively you can click Ctrl+A to sort the entire spreadsheet.

2. Click Data | Sort... The Sort dialog box will open.

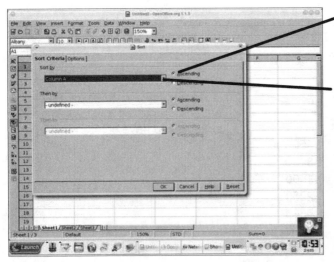

3. Click the radio button beside the desired sorting option. You can choose either ascending or descending.

4. Click the drop-down menu and choose the criteria to sort. Typically this is the column title that you would like to sort.

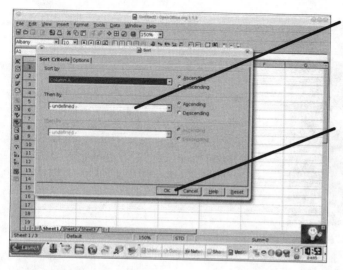

5. Repeat Steps 3 and 4 in the "Then by" areas for secondary and tertiary sort options. In other words, after the first sort option is selected, what is the second and third sorting criteria that should be followed.

6. Click OK. The dialog box will close and your sort will be conducted.

# AutoFilter

Who says that sliced bread was the greatest invention? Rather than sorting your data, AutoFilter automatically filters out information from your spreadsheet based on criteria that you set. Little menus will appear from which you can select criteria to filter your data. We'll use the example of a soccer team. If I had a spreadsheet of an entire league and wanted to filter the data to find certain similarities, for example, see only the people who were on a specific team, AutoFilter allows me to do this at the click of a mouse button.

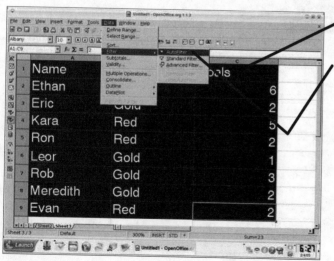

1. Click and drag across the cells that you would like to AutoFilter.

2. Click Data | Filter | AutoFilter. Little arrows will appear at the edge of the top cells in your selection. These are pop-up menus that can be used to filter your data.

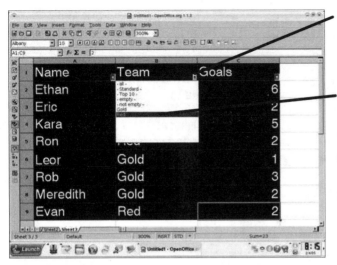

3. Click any of the AutoFilter arrows. A list of contents that can be filtered will appear, along with a few other options.

4. Click the desired criteria that you want to filter. In this example, I want to see only those people that are on the Red team and filter out the rest, so I click Red. The spreadsheet will filter out everything but the criteria that I selected.

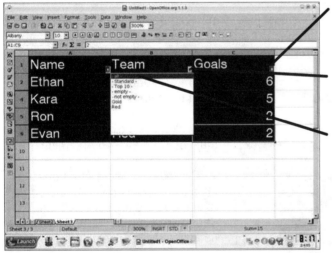

5. Repeat Steps 4 and 5 for any other columns that you would like to filter.

6. Click any of the AutoFilter arrows that you have previously filtered. The list will reappear.

7. Click All. The filter will be removed and all of the data within the column will reappear, unless there is a filter on another column preventing the data from being shown.

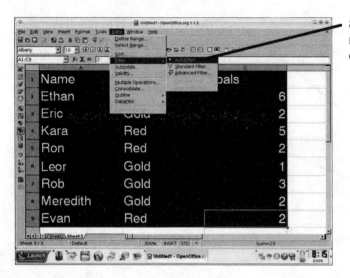

8.  Click Data | Filter | AutoFilter to remove AutoFilter and return your document to its pre-filtered state.

# AutoFill

When creating spreadsheets there are certain strings of text that you typically have to create over and over.  Examples of these include, days of the week, months, and numbered lists.  To help you complete these tasks even faster Spreadsheet has an AutoFill tool which allows you to enter only the first part of a string, and Spreadsheet will do the rest.  For example, if you wanted to create a sheet with the days of the week, you would only have to type Monday, the rest of the days could be AutoFilled.

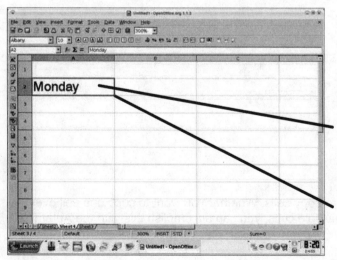

## Basic AutoFills

For simple AutoFills you can enter a value, then click and drag.

1.  Type the first value for the string you want to create.  This can be any number or certain words including days of the week, months or dates.

2.  Position the mouse pointer over the bottom right corner of a cell.  The mouse pointer will turn into a small plus sign.

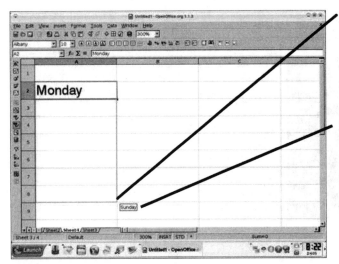

3. Click and drag in the direction where you want the rest of the string to appear. In this example, we are dragging downwards to enter the different days of the week in the first column.

4. Take note of the tool tip that appears as you drag. The will tell you the content final cell of your string.

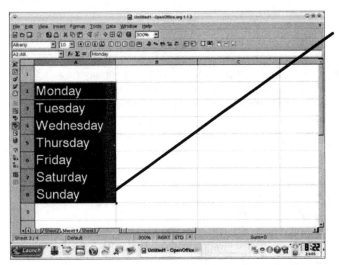

5. Release the mouse button. The cells you dragged over will automatically be filled.

# Copying with AutoFill

Another handy use of AutoFill is to copy cells. Whether you want to copy one cell over and over or if you want to copy multiple cells, you can accomplish this with the AutoFill.

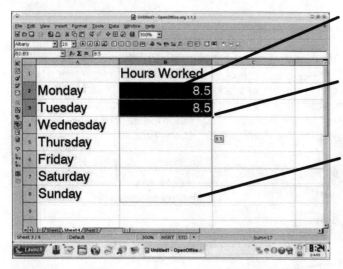

1. Click and drag across the cell or cells that you would like to copy. They will be highlighted.

2. Position the mouse pointer at the bottom right corner of the cells that you would like to copy. The mouse pointer will turn into a little plus sign.

3. Click and drag over the destination cells where you want to copy your selection.

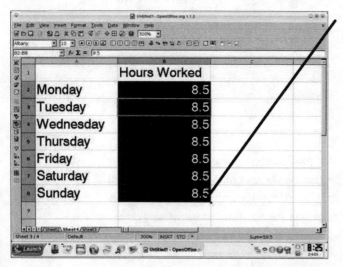

4. Release the mouse button. The selection will be copied to the selected rows. If the area you selected in Step 3 was greater than your original selection, the selection will repeat once copied.

*Typical editing features like copying, cutting, pasting and undoing are the same across the OpenOffice suite. Refer to the last chapter to review using these features.*

# Formatting Worksheets

Let's face it, numbers scare people. A spreadsheet full of numerical data can be quite intimidating to the faint of heart. To alleviate some of the fear that people face when encountering a spreadsheet, you can format your worksheet in a variety of different ways. Through formatting you can emphasize certain areas or points, make data more understandable and accessible and change the overall appearance of your spreadsheet. Most formatting features can be found in the Format Cells dialog box.

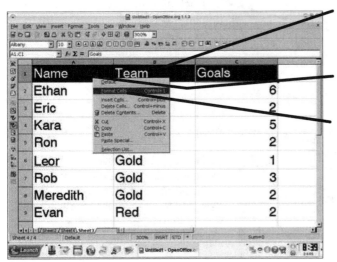

1. Select the cells that you want to apply a color to using one of the selection methods.

2. Right-click anywhere on your selection. A menu will appear.

3. Click Format Cells...The Format Cells dialog box will open.

*Many of the formatting features discussed in the section below can also be accessed from the toolbar. Hover your mouse pointer over any button in the toolbar to see what it does.*

# Applying Colors to Cells

One of the best ways to make your data easier to understand is to apply colors to the cells in your spreadsheet.

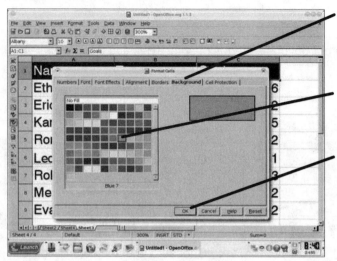

1.  Click on the Background tab.  You will be presented with a palette of colors to select as the cell background.

2.  Click the color that you want to apply.  A preview of the color will appear in the dialog box.

3.  Click OK.  The Format Cells dialog box will close and your selection will be colored.

## Wrapping and Rotating Text

If you enter text into a cell that is longer than the width of the cell, the text will be cut off by any content in the cell beside it.  To avoid this you can select the wrap cell feature.  Just like in a word processor, when text reaches the width of the cell, it will flow to another line with text wrapping activated.  You can also rotate text within a cell.

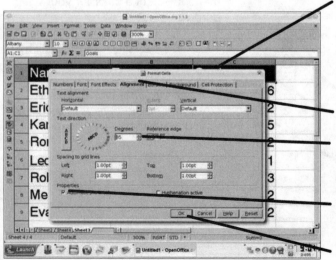

1.  Select the cells that you want to edit. They will be highlighted.

2.  Open the Format Cells dialog box as discussed in the "Formatting Worksheets" section earlier.

3.  Click on the Alignment tab.

4.  Click on the up and down arrows to change the degree of rotation for the text in the cell.

5.  Click on the Automatic line break check box so that text will wrap.

6.  Click OK.  The effect is applied.

## Borders

Spreadsheet offers a range of border options, in terms of both styles and thicknesses that you can apply to your selections.

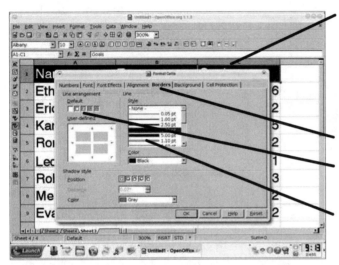

1.  Select the cell(s) that you want to apply a border to using one of the selection methods.

2.  Open the Format Cells dialog box as discussed in the "Formatting Worksheets" section earlier.

3.  Click on the Borders tab.

4.  Choose one of the default border types.

5.  Click on the desired line thickness for your cell.

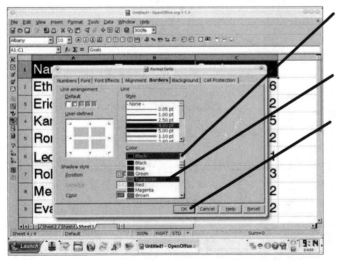

6.  Click on the color drop-down menu to select a color for your border.

7.  Click the desired color. It will be selected.

8.  Click OK. The dialog box will close and the borders will be applied to your selection.

# Numerical Formatting

Do you remember 5th Grade math class where you had to learn how to round up or down to two decimal places? If only you had Spreadsheet which could do it for you automatically. Spreadsheet has a variety of preset numerical formats that you can apply to your cells. Any data that you enter into those formatted cells will take on the numerical formatting that you have selected. For example, if you have formatted a cell to be three decimal places and then enter the number 4.56768, the number will appear as 4.677.

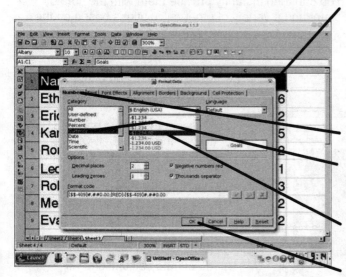

1. Select the cell(s) to which you want to apply numerical formatting using one of the selection methods.

2. Open the Format Cells dialog box as discussed in the "Formatting Worksheets" section earlier.

3. Click on the Numbers tab.

4. Click on the desired category of the type of number you are formatting.

5. Click the desired format from the samples of formats that appear.

6. Click OK. The numerical formatting will be applied and the dialog box will close.

*There are dozens of other formatting features that you can apply to your cells. You should explore the Format Cells dialog box to experiment with other formatting options.*

# Formulas and Other Math

The real power or Spreadsheet is that you can enter formulas, change your data, and then quickly see the changes in the results of your formulas.

## AutoCalculate

Here's a way for you to impress your friends at parties. Have them gather around your computer and call out numbers. You can then instantly provide them with the sum of those numbers, the average, the count and a variety of other calculations based on the numbers they've provided. There's no need for a Mensa membership to perform this trick, it's as simple as highlighting the numbers.

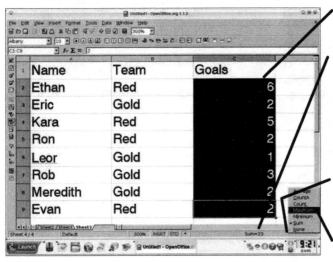

1. Create a selection of numbers that you want to find the sum for.

2. Observe the status bar at the bottom of the screen. It will automatically provide you with the sum of those numbers. If you don't want to find the sum, there are a variety of other calculations that can be done instantly.

3. Right-click on the status bar. A menu of auto calculations will appear.

4. Click on the desired calculation including:

- Average. This will display the mean or average of your selection.

- Count. This will indicate the total number of cells that are selected.

- CountA. This will indicate the total number of cells that contain numbers that are selected.

- Max. This will display the maximum number in the selection.

- Min. This will display the lowest number in the selection.

- Sum. This will show the sum of all the numbers in the selection.

# AutoSum

The most common formula entered in Spreadsheet is sum, or in other words, adding up a series of cells. Since this is such a common formula, the good folks at OpenOffice have made it easy for you to calculate a sum by creating a button that will insert the formula for you. This button is called AutoSum and will instantly calculate the sum of a selection

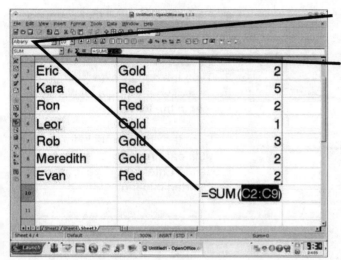

1. Click on a cell below or to the right of the cells that you would like to add.

2. Click the AutoSum button. A formula will appear in the cell and a blue outline will appear around the cells to be added.

3. Press the Enter key on the keyboard or click the Accept button. The cells will be added and the results will appear in the cell you selected.

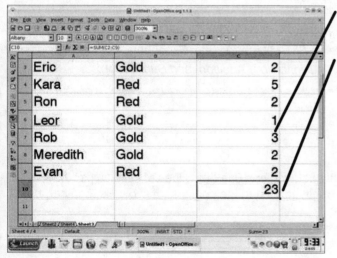

4. Change any of the numbers that were added.

5. Observe the results. The results will automatically update to reflect the changes that you made to the data.

# Formulas

There are countless formulas that you can enter into your spreadsheet to perform calculations. All formulas have one thing in common: they all begin with an operator, an equals sign (=). An operator tells Spreadsheet that the content of the cell is a formula and not a label.

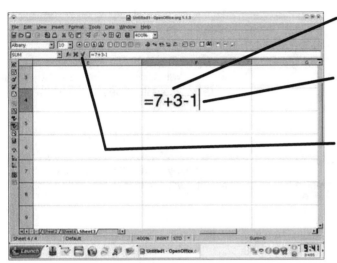

1. Click once in a cell that you would like to add a formula to. The cell will be highlighted.

2. Type the equals sign (=) then type the rest of your formula. It will appear in the formula bar.

3. Click the check mark in the formula bar (the Accept button) or press the Enter key. The formula will be inserted into the cell.

*The rules of order of operation apply when creating formulas in Spreadsheet. Remember the order is BEDMAS: Brackets, Exponents, Division, Multiplication, Addition, and Subtraction.*

# Cell References

When creating formulas in Spreadsheet, you can use the values of cells as part of your equations. In this example we'll simply add 3 and the contents of two cells together, but you can enter any formula.

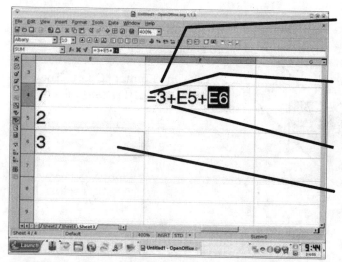

1.  Click once on the cell where you would like the results of your calculation to be displayed.

2.  Click the equals sign to begin the formula and type the number 3. It will appear in the formula bar.

3.  Type the plus sign (+). It will appear after the 3 in the formula bar.

4.  Click on a cell you would like to include in your formula. It will have a red outline.

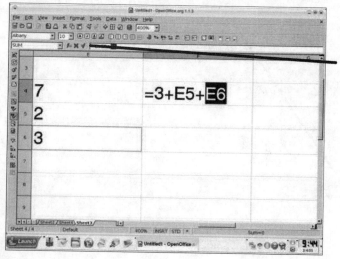

5.  Repeat Steps 4 - 5 to add any other cells to the formula.

6.  Click the Accept button to complete the formula.

# Charts

If there's a better visual than a pie chart, I haven't seen it. The ability to convert your data from boring, senseless numbers to visual masterpieces is the real power of Spreadsheet. There are dozens of options when it comes to creating graphs (more commonly referred to as charts) in Spreadsheet. The beauty of the program is that stunning graphical representations of your data can be created in seconds with a few clicks of the mouse button.

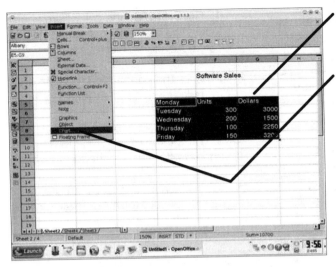

1. Select the data you would like represented in a graph using one of the selection methods.

2. Click the Format | Chart. The AutoFormat Chart wizard will appear.

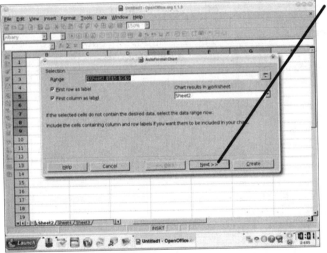

3. Click the Next button to proceed to the next stage in the wizard.

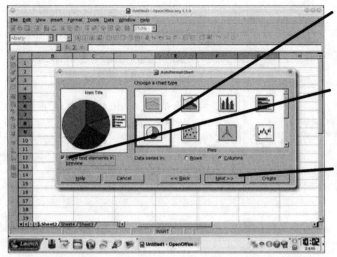

4. Click on the type of graph that you would like to create. A preview of that type of graph will appear in the display.

5. Click on the Show text elements in preview check box if you want to see how the text labels will appear in the graph.

6. Click the Next button to move to the next stage.

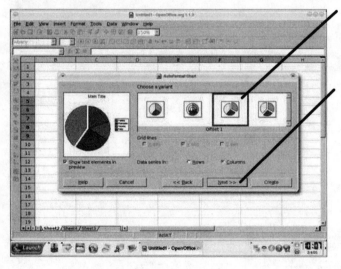

7. Click on a variant of the graph if so desired. This gives you additional options for the graph you've selected.

8. Click the Next button to move to the next stage.

*You don't have to complete every step of the AutoFormat Chart wizard. You can click on the Create button at any time to finish the graph.*

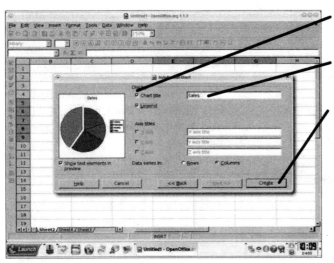

9. Click the check boxes to include what to display.

10. Type in the desired text for the titles and axis as needed.

11. Click the Create button. The graph will be inserted in your spreadsheet.

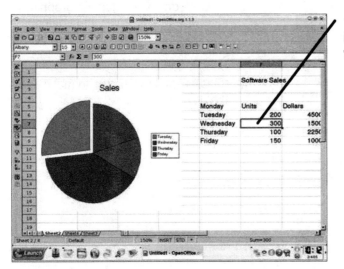

12. Change any of the values represented in the chart. The chart will change to reflect those changes.

# Creating Graphics & Slide Shows

**7**

Within the OpenOffice suite that comes with your Linspire computer, you'll find a program called Drawings. This program allows you to not only create graphical images, but also, present those graphics as slide shows. The program itself is actually quite advanced and has literally hundreds of different features you can use when creating your images. It would take an entire book to cover all of the features, so in this chapter we'll concentrate on the basics and try to also show you a few advanced features.

You may also notice that there is another program in the Launch menu, under the OpenOffice group called Presentations. This program is actually the same as Drawings, with the exception that it starts with a wizard to create a slide show. This wizard is accessible from within Drawings and will be covered in detail within this chapter.

In this chapter we'll cover:

- Building and playing a slide show
- Creating graphical elements
- Editing and manipulating objects

# Launching Drawings

Drawings can be found in the Launch menu along with the rest of the OpenOffice suite.

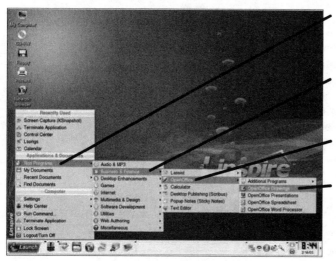

1. Click Launch | Run Programs. A list of programs categories will appear.

2. Click Business & Finance to see a list of programs that fall under that category.

3. Click OpenOffice. The OpenOffice programs will appear.

4. Click OpenOffice Drawings. The program will launch.

# Building a Slide Show

Here's some rocket science for you – a slide show is built of individual slides. The slides themselves can include text, graphics, movies and audio. For now we'll cover how to add and remove slides and how to use the wizard to automatically create a slide show.

## Using AutoPilot

If you're just not graphically inclined or don't want to spend a lot of time formatting your slide show, you can choose from a several different design templates. These design templates usually include formatting for backgrounds, fonts and colors. Using the AutoPilot wizard not only can you select a design template, but you can also build the content of your slide show. The wizard will ask you a variety of questions about what you want to include in your slides and upon answering those questions, the slide show will be built for you.

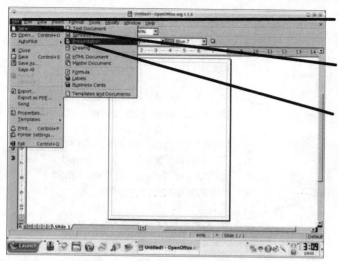

1. Click File. The File menu appears.

2. Click New. A submenu will expand.

3. Click Presentation. The AutoPilot Presentation window will appear. You can use this wizard to build your slide show.

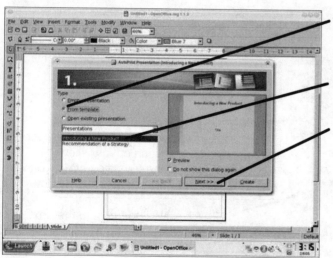

4. Click on the radio button beside From template. This will allow you to select a template in the next step.

5. Click on the desired template. It will be highlighted.

6. Click the Next button to move to the next page of the AutoPilot.

*You don't have to complete every step of the AutoPilot Presentation wizard. You can click on the Create button at any time to finish the presentation based on the info you've given so far.*

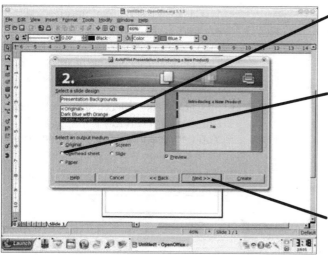

7.  Click on the desired slide design template.  It will be highlighted and a preview of the design will appear in the window.

8.  Click on the radio button beside the desired output for the slide show.  This will help determine the settings from the layout of the slide show.  Those designed to be printed will be formatted differently then those designed for on-screen.

9.  Click Next to move to the next stage of the AutoPilot wizard.

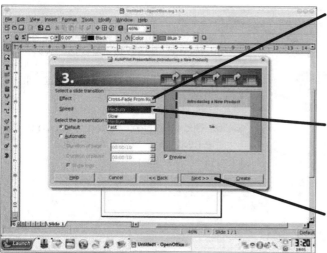

10.  Click the drop-down arrow beside Effect and click on a desired effect for the transition of your slides.  A preview of the transition effect that you selected will appear in the window.

11.  Click the drop-down arrow beside Speed and click on the speed for the transition of your slides.  A preview of the transition effect you selected will appear in the window.

12.  Click Next to move to the next stage of the AutoPilot wizard.

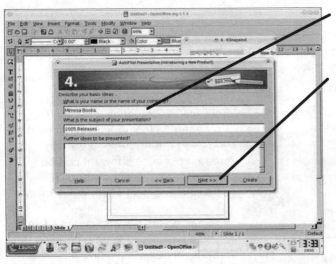

13. Type in the desired information about your presentation in the fields provided.

14. Click Next to proceed to the pages section of the wizard.

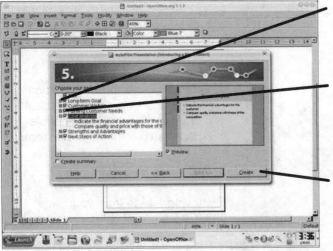

15. Click on the + beside any page to view its contents. These are the headings that you'll see on the pages when you create the slide show.

16. Click the check box beside any of the pages that you want to include. Keep in mind that these pages can be completely customized after the slide show has been created.

17. Click Create. The slides show will be created based on the information that you have entered into the wizard.

*A slide show can be played at any time by pressing the F9 key. While it is playing, pressing any key will advance to the next slide. Pressing the Esc key will exit your slide show.*

# Creating Slides

Whenever you add a slide you are given a choice as to its layout. You can select from a variety of layouts or choose a blank slide.

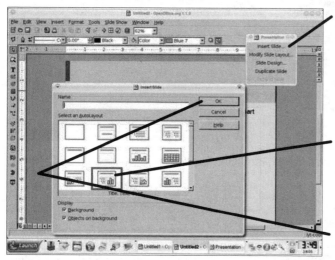

1.  Click the Insert Slide... button from the Presentation toolbar. The Presentation toolbar is only present if you used the AutoPilot wizard to create your slide show. It can be opened from the View menu by selecting Toolbars | Presentation.

2.  Click on the desired layout. The layouts typically include a heading, a graphic, a table, a picture, a bulleted list, or some combination of those elements.

3.  Click OK. The slide you selected will be added to the slide show.

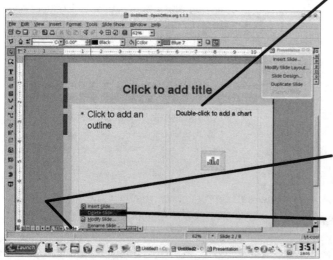

4.  Follow the on-screen instructions for adding the elements to the slide you created. Typically you double-click in an area to add that element.

## Deleting a Slide

Removing a slide from your slide show is a piece of cake.

1.  Right-click on the name of the slide you would like to delete. A menu will appear.

2.  Click Delete Slide... A dialog box will open confirming that you would like to delete the slide. Click Yes when that dialog box appears.

# Switching Slides

The quickest way to switch from one slide to another is to simply click on the name of the slide you would like to move to.

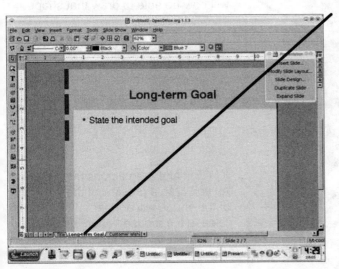

1. Click on the name of the slide you would like to move to. You will now be taken to that slide.

# Creating Graphical Elements

Whether you are going to be using the graphics you create on their own or as part of a slide show, Drawing gives you a variety of tools that you can use to create some amazing, visually appealing graphics.

# Inserting Shapes

Drawing provides you with tools to quickly add a variety of preset shapes to your slide show. If you're not satisfied with the shapes that are included, you can always draw your own.

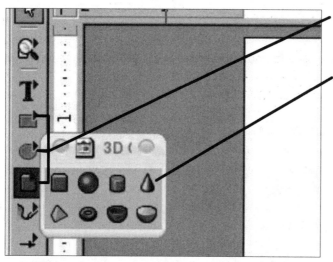

1. Click and hold any of the three shape buttons. A menu of different shapes will appear.

2. Click on the desired shape. You will now be able to draw that shape across the page.

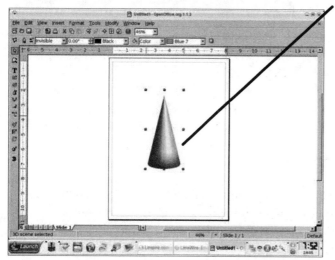

3. Click and drag across the page. As you drag a preview of the location of the shape will appear. When you release the mouse button the shape will appear on your page.

## Connector Lines

Commonly Drawings is used to illustrate an organizational chart. Most organizational charts are simply a matter of boxes that are connected with lines. Drawings allows you to create lines that dynamically link to objects. This means that if you move an object with a dynamically linked line attached to it, the line will move along with the object. If you'd prefer to create regular lines and arrows, you can do so using the same method as for drawing shapes that was discussed in the last section.

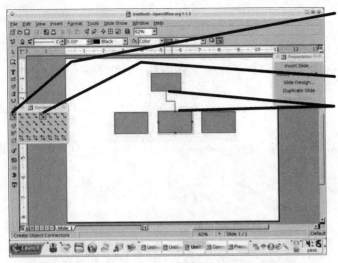

1. Click and hold the Connectors button to see a list of connection lines.

2. Click on the desired type of line.

3. Click and drag from one object to the other. The connector line will be created between the two objects. The objects are now dynamically linked, meaning if you move either object, the line will still connect them.

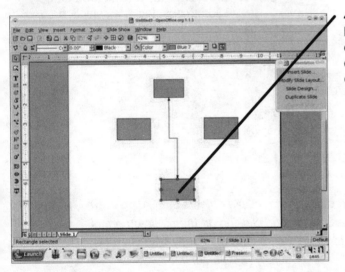

4. Click and drag one of the objects bound by a connector line to a different part of the page. The objects will still be linked as the connector line adjusts.

## Editing Graphical Elements

Basic things like copying, cutting and pasting work the same way in Drawings as they do for other parts of the suite. You do have several unique options though when it comes to selecting, moving and resizing graphical elements.

# Selecting Objects

As with most features in Drawings you have a variety of different options when it comes to making selections. Making selections is the cornerstone to editing, as an object must be selected before anything can be done to it.

## Selecting Individual Objects

To select individual objects you simply have to click on them.

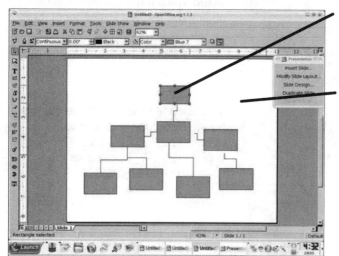

1. Click once on an object. A series of little green squares will appear around the object indicating that it is selected.

2. Click on any blank area of the slide to deselect the selection.

*You can select multiple objects by holding down the Ctrl key and clicking on them. If you press Ctrl+A on the keyboard, all the objects on the screen will be selected.*

## Selecting Multiple Objects

The advantage of selecting multiple objects is that you can save time by editing many objects at once. To select multiple objects, you have to create a marquee selection around your objects.

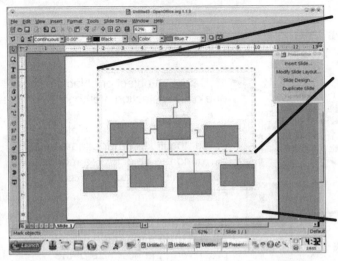

1.  Position your mouse pointer in a blank area to the top left of the objects that you want to select.

2.  Click and drag diagonally.  As you drag a marquee will appear.  The marquee must completely surround the objects that you would like to select. When you release the mouse button all of the objects that were completely surrounded by the marquee will be selected.

3.  Click once in any blank area of the slide show to deselect your selection.

# Moving Objects

Moving objects is simply a matter of selecting them and then dragging them to the desired location.

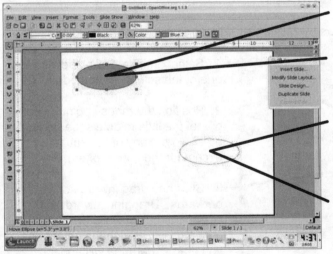

1.  Select an object or objects using one of the selection methods.

2.  Position the mouse pointer over the object.  The mouse pointer will change into a four-sided arrow.

3.  Click and drag the object to the desired location.  As you drag, a transparent preview of the location of the objects will appear.

4.  Release the mouse button.  The objects will be moved.

# Resizing Objects

Once you have an object selected you can quickly change its size or reshape it.

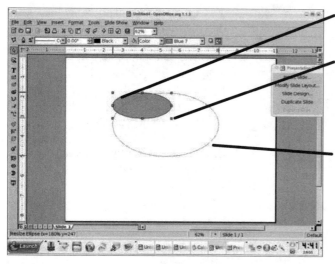

1. Select an object or objects using one of the selection methods.

2. Position the mouse pointer over one of the little corner squares that surround the object. The mouse pointer will turn into a two-sided arrow.

3. Click and drag in any direction. As you drag a marquee will appear previewing the new size of the object. When you release the mouse button the object will be resized.

# Squishing and Stretching Objects

You can squish or stretch an object by clicking and dragging on any of its middle handles.

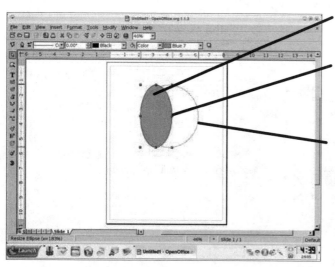

1. Select an object or objects using one of the selection methods.

2. Position the mouse pointer over one of the little middle squares (in other words, any of the squares except for the corner ones).

3. Click and drag inwards or outwards. Dragging inwards will squish the object while dragging outwards will stretch the object. As you drag a marquee will appear previewing the new shape of the object. When you release the mouse button the object will be reshaped.

# Colors, Fills and Outlines

What's better than a rectangle?  A rectangle with some color!  You can add colors, patterns and change line fills for your objects.

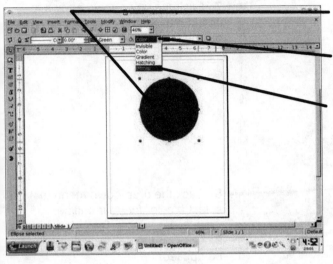

1.  Select the object or objects that you would like to apply a fill to.

2.  Click the Fill drop-down menu.  A list of types of fills will appear.

3.  Click the desired fill your options include:

- Invisible.  Removes the fill.

- Color.  Creates a solid-colored fill.

- Gradient. Creates a multi-colored fill.

- Hatching. Creates a patterned fill.

- Bitmap.  Inserts a picture of a pattern.

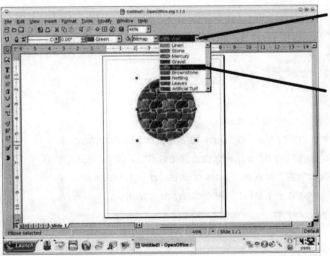

4.  Click on the drop-down for the Areas Style/Filing.  A variety of fills for the type of fill you selected will appear.

5.  Click the desired fill. It will be applied to the selected object.

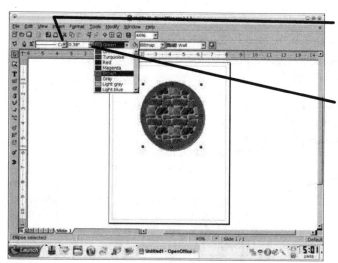

6. Click the drop-down menu and select an outline style for your object if you don't want the outline to be a solid line.

7. Click the up or down arrows to adjust the width of the object's outline.

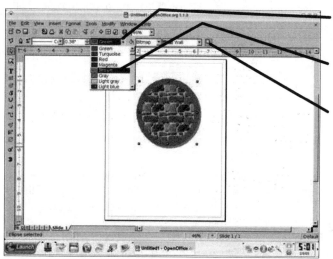

8. Click the drop-down menu to select a color for your outline.

9. Click on the desired color. It will be applied.

10. Click on the shadow button to give your object a shadow.

*Holding down the Shift key while you are creating or resizing an object will constrain the horizontal and vertical motion. This is great if you want to create symmetrical circles or squares.*

# Working with Text

Most of your slides will contain text in one form or the other. There are so many things that can be done to text to make it stand out.

## Adding Text

To add text to a slide you must create a text box. A text box is a container for your text that helps you organize how text appears on your slide. The Text box tool can be found in the Drawing toolbar.

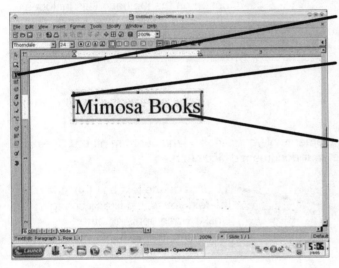

1. Click the Text tool. It will be highlighted.

2. Click once at the approximate location you would like the text to appear. A text box will be created and the cursor will be flashing within.

3. Begin typing. The text will appear in the text box that you have created.

## Formatting Text

Most of the formatting tools that can be applied to text can be found in the toolbar. To format text, the text itself must be selected. This means you must first select the text box and then click and drag across the text that you would like to format. Once you have text selected it is easily formatted.

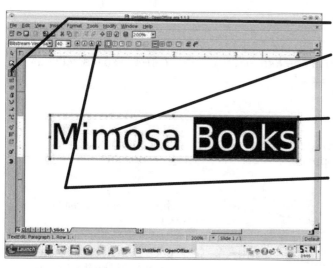

1. Click the Text tool in the toolbox.

2. Double-click on the text that you would like to format. The cursor will now be in the text box.

3. Click and drag across the text that you would like to format. It will be highlighted.

4. Click on the desired formatting option on the toolbar. This includes selecting font face, size, justification and spacing.

## Font Color

Using color you can make certain elements of your slides stand out from others. Keep in mind that certain colors may make your document difficult to read.

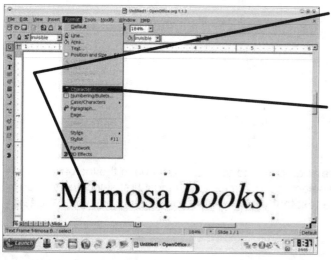

1. Click on the text box that contains the text you would like to change. Unlike when applying other formatting, don't double-click on the box to bring up the cursor.

2. Click Format | Character... The Character dialog box will appear.

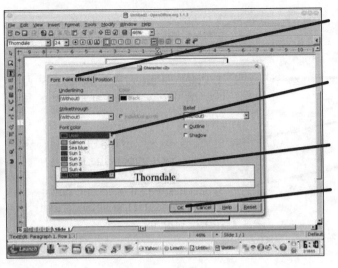

3. Click on the Font Effects tab. You'll now see a variety of font effects.

4. Click the drop-down menu to see a list of colors from which you can select.

5. Click on the desired color. It will be selected.

6. Click OK. The color will change.

# Fontwork

The Fontwork feature in Drawings allows you to apply a variety of preset effects to your text. It's really the easiest way to create some outstanding effects to your text, with very little effort.

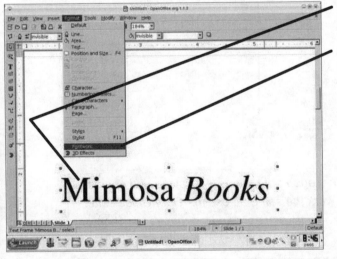

1. Click on the text that you would like to apply the effect to.

2. Click Format | Fontwork. The Fontwork dialog box appears.

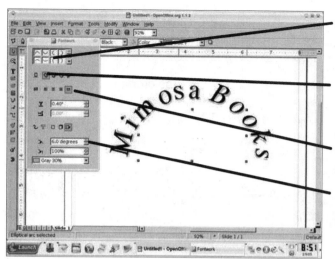

3. Click on the desired shape. The text will be wrapped in the shape you selected.

4. Click on the option for how you'd like the text wrapped around the shape.

5. Click on any of the other options to test how it affects the text.

6. Click any of the up and down arrows to adjust the settings that you've applied.

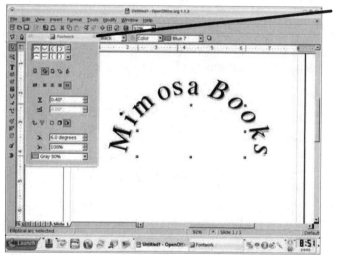

7. Click the Close button in the top right corner of the Fontwork window to close it.

*File management options like saving and opening files work the same across the OpenOffice suite. To review these commands, examine the chapter entitled "Word Processing."*

# Using Multimedia Programs

It's amazing how far computers have come over the last few years. I remember as a kid growing up we got so excited when our local museum opened a computer wing. You could go into that section, and you could play Pong (a very simple tennis-like game for those of you who've never heard of it). You could also answer a yes or no question posed by the computer and it would do a psychological analysis of you or you could type in your birthday and get your biorhythm. Fast-forward to today, where you can download and view your favorite music videos, burn CDs, manipulate photos, watch DVDs, play interactive games and do so much more.

No operating system would be worth its weight in salt if it didn't give you access to your favorite multimedia components, and Linspire is no slouch in this department. Right out of the box you are provided with a full range of multimedia tools that are at your disposal to keep you entertained.

In this chapter we'll cover:

- Playing music with Lsongs
- Using Lphoto to manipulate photos
- Downloading photos from a digital camera

# Using Lsongs

Lsongs is a comprehensive program that allows you to manage and play your favorite mp3 and other audio songs. You can also pretend to be your own program director at a radio station, as you can create custom playlists. And speaking of radio, Lsongs allows you to listen to a range of Internet-based radio stations. Lsongs comes pre-installed on your Linspire computer and can be accessed from the Launch menu.

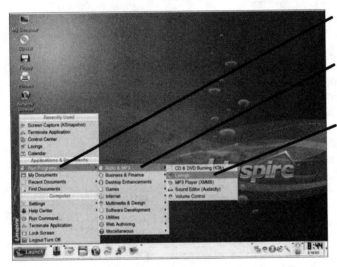

1. Click Launch | Run Programs. A list of program categories will appear.

2. Click Audio & MP3 to reveal the programs that fall within that category.

3. Click Lsongs. The Lsongs program will launch.

## Adding Songs

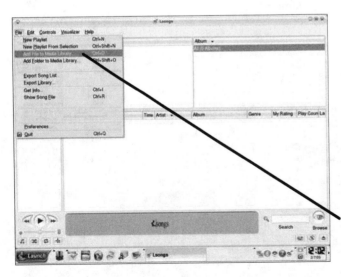

Before you can begin playing your mp3 files, you'll need to add them to the media library in Lsongs. You can select individual files to import, entire folders, or CDs.

### Adding Individual Songs

To add songs to the media library one at a time you can simply browse your computer's hard drive.

1. Click File | Add File to Media Library… A dialog box will appear from which you can select your files.

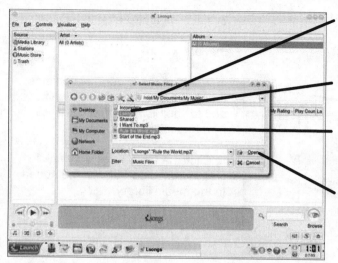

2.  Navigate to the folder that contains the songs that you would like to add to your media library.

3.  Click on the desired song. It will be highlighted.

4.  Hold down the Ctrl key and click on any other songs in the folder that you would like to add.

5.  Click the Open button. The files you selected will be added to your media library.

## Adding Entire Folders

Most people keep all of their music files within one or two folders, so Lsongs rewards those among us that keep organized by allowing to you add all the songs within a folder to your media library. When you select a folder to add, Lsongs will search through that folder, select the music files and then import them into the media library.

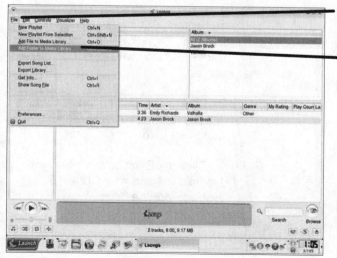

1.  Click File. The File menu will appear.

2.  Click Add Folder to Media Library... A dialog box will appear from which you can select the folder that contains music files.

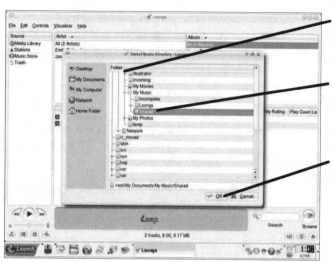

3.  Click on a plus sign to expand a folder in order to see the subfolders that are within.

4.  Click on the folder that contains the music files that you would like to add to your library. The folder will now be highlighted.

5. Click the OK button. Any music files in that folder will now be added to the media library.

## Importing Songs from a CD

The process of creating mp3 files from CDs is commonly referred to as ripping. Although it is possible to play your CDs in Lsongs without first converting them to mp3s, the tracks cannot be added to the media library unless they are made into mp3s. The process of converting CD tracks to mp3s is just a matter of one click of the mouse button.

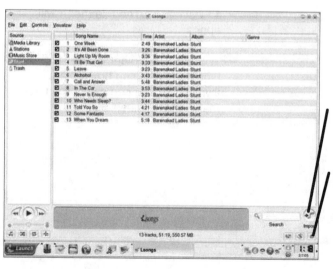

1.  Insert your CD into your computer's CD drive. After a moment, Lsongs will load all of the tracks and they will appear on the screen.

2.  Click the Import button. Lsongs will convert the tracks to mp3's and add them to the media library.

3.  Click the Eject button when you are finished and your CD will be ejected from the drive.

# Playing Songs

Once you have your songs loaded into the media library you can play them by double-clicking on any song.

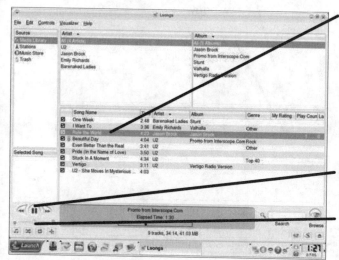

1. Double-click on any song that you would like to play. The song will begin to play. When the song reaches the end, the next song in your list that has a check mark in the box to its left will play. You'll learn more about controlling which songs play and in what order in the next section.

2. Click the Pause button at any time to pause the playback.

3. Click and drag the volume slider to adjust the volume. Dragging to the left decreases the volume and dragging to the right increases it.

*Holding down the Ctrl key and pressing the right arrow key will play the next song in the list. Pressing the left arrow key with the Ctrl key held down will play the previous song.*

# Finding and Organizing Music

Mp3s are popular, very popular, and really why not? They don't scratch, they're cheap, they're widely available and they are very portable. Whether you convert your existing CD collection to mp3s or purchase your files, there's a good possibility that your collection will grow into the hundreds if not the thousands. That could pose a problem, if not for the many organizing features available in Lsongs. The beauty of mp3s is that you can associate information like the artist, album, genre and title to the file, which makes for easy searching and organizing. By default, Lsongs categorizes your music by the information provided in the file so that you can quickly find what you're looking for.

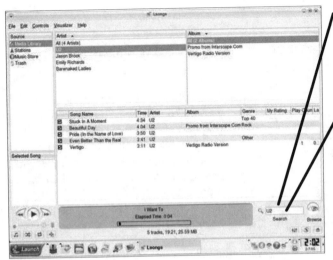

1. Type the name of a song, artist or album that you are looking for into the Search box. As you type, all of the results that match your search terms will be displayed in the window.

2. Delete the search term to return to your full list.

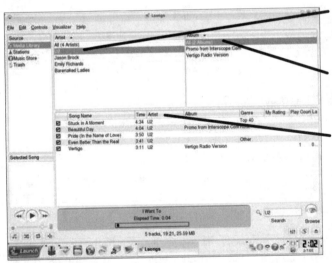

3. Click on an artist. All of the songs by that artist will appear in the song list.

4. Click on an album. All the songs in your list that belong to that album will appear.

5. Click on a heading in the song list area. The list will be sorted based on the title that you selected. For example if you clicked the Artist heading, the songs would be rearranged by artist in alphabetical order.

## Adding Data to Music Files

Depending on where you obtained your mp3 files from, they may not contain all of the correct information associated with the file. Lsongs allows you to add a variety of information to your mp3 files, even such things as genres and album covers. The more accurate the information you have on your files, the easier it will be to find and sort.

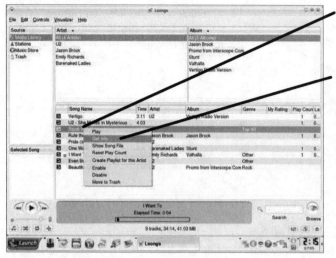

1. Right-click on any file to which you would like to add information. A menu will appear.

2. Click Get Info... A dialog box will appear where you can enter all types of information about your song.

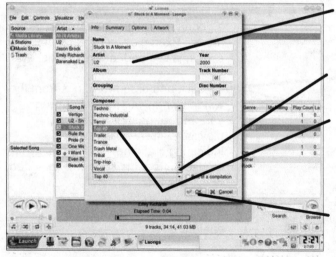

3. Type in any information that you know about the file into the fields provided.

4. Click the drop-down arrow and select a genre for this song file.

5. Explore the other tabs to see what other information you can add. If you want to add an album cover you can click on the Artwork tab and explore that option.

6. Click the OK button when you have completed adding information to the file.

# Playlists

I remember when I was in high school, if a guy wanted to impress a girl he would make a mix tape of her favorite songs. You can create your own "mix tapes" in Lsongs (called playlists), that include particular songs that you would like to hear in a certain order. You can create playlists that reflect certain moods, types of music, artists, albums or genres.

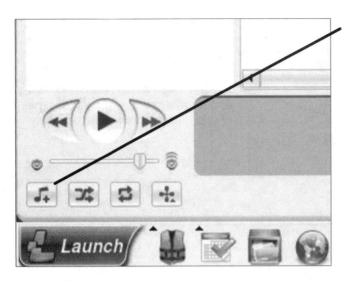

1. Click the Add Playlist button. You will now be prompted to type a name for your playlist.

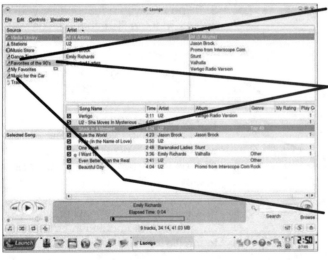

2. Type a name for your playlist. It is a good idea to give it a descriptive name. Examples include: my favorite songs, jazz blend, driving music, etc.

3. Click and drag any songs from the window onto your playlist. When your mouse pointer is over the playlist, a little + will appear, indicating that when you release your mouse button, the song will be added to the playlist.

4. Click on any Playlist to reveal its contents.

## Creating CD's from Playlists

Just as you could convert audio CD's to mp3's, the opposite is also true. After you've created a playlist, you can burn the contents of that playlist to an audio CD that you can play in your car or home stereo.

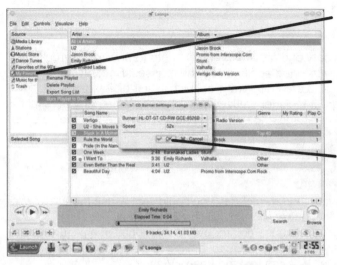

1.  Right-click on any playlist that you would like to create an audio CD from. A menu will appear.

2.  Click Burn Playlist to Disc.

3.  Insert your writeable CD into the CD burner.

4.  Click OK. Your playlist will be converted to audio files and be burnt to the CD. It now can be played like any other audio CD.

# Internet Radio

There are a variety of Internet-based radio stations that you can listen to directly from your Linspire computer. Whether it's easy listening, hard rock or classical, there's a good chance you'll find an Internet radio station to meet your musical tastes.

1.  Click the Stations button. The Shoutcast page will appear.

2.  Type the particular station you are looking for in the search box. You can search by station, song, genre or artist. Alternatively you can scroll through the different stations until you find one you like.

3.  Click the Go! button. A list of stations that match your search criteria will appear.

4.  Click the Tune In button beside the station you'd like to hear. The radio station will begin to play through your computer speakers.

# Working with Photos

Over the last five years, the popularity and growth of digital photography has skyrocketed. This is how you know a technology is being accepted by the masses: Both my mother and my mother in law both have - and are quite proficient with - their digital cameras. Linspire comes with a couple of great tools for working with photos. Whether you're just looking to view pictures or want to manage and edit your photos, Linspire has the solution for you.

## Viewing Photos

Technically speaking, if you just want to view pictures you could simply use the File Manger in Thumbnail view mode. If you recall from the chapter entitled "File Management," if you simply hover your mouse pointer over a thumbnail of a picture you would see an enlarged version of your photo. If you're looking for a method of viewing photos that is a little more functional, you can use the Image Viewer.

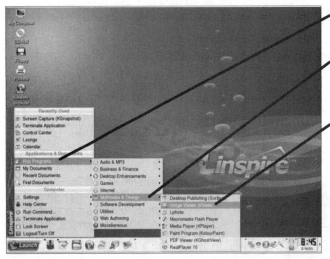

1. Click Launch | Run Programs. You'll now see a list of categories.

2. Click Multimedia & Design to see a list of programs that fall under that category.

3. Click Image Viewer. The Image Viewer will launch.

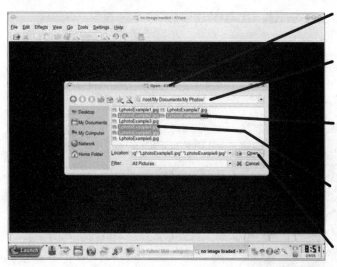

4.  Press Ctrl+O on your keyboard. The Open dialog box will appear.

5.  Navigate to the folder that contains the photo that you would like to open.

6.  Click on one of the photos that you would like to open. It will be highlighted.

7.  Hold down the Ctrl key and continue clicking other image files. They too will now be highlighted.

8.  Click the Open button. The photos will be loaded into the image viewer.

9.  Click View | Fit Image to Window. The image will be enlarged to fit the entire space of the window.

10.  Press S on the keyboard to begin a slide show of your images.

11.  Press S again on your keyboard to end the slide show of your images.

*If you prefer to manually toggle between your photos, you can use the keyboard. Alt+right arrow moves to the next image and Alt+left arrow takes you to the previous image.*

## Managing and Editing Photos with Lphoto

While the Image Viewer allows you to quickly view your images, Lphoto is a much more powerful tool to help you view, manage and edit your photographs. When you first launch Lphoto, a wizard will appear that will scan the "My Photos" folder on your computer, looking for photos, that it will then add to the Photo Library.

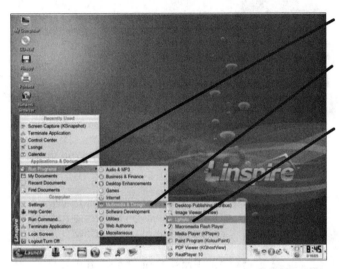

1. Click Launch | Run Programs. A list of program categories will appear.

2. Click Multimedia & Design. A submenu of different programs appears.

3. Click Lphoto. The program will launch.

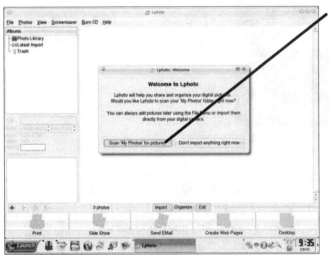

4. Click the "Scan 'My Photos' for pictures" button. Lphoto will look to you're my Photos folder on your system. Alternatively, you can click the "Don't import anything right now" button if you'd like to manually add photos to your library later. All the pictures in you're my Photos folder will now appear in the window. A dialog box will appear asking you whether you want to delete your images from the original location as Lphoto has made a copy of the images to be included in the Photo Library.

5. Click the No button. It's always a good idea to leave a copy of your images in their original location.

6. Double-click on any photo to see an enlarged version of the photo.

7. Click the Photo Library button to return to the thumbnail view.

## Creating Albums

Think of the Photo Library as one large album that contains all of your photographs. Rather then having to keep all of your photos in one large album, you can create individual albums to make it easier to view and sort your photos. Adding photos to the albums you create is simply a matter of clicking and dragging.

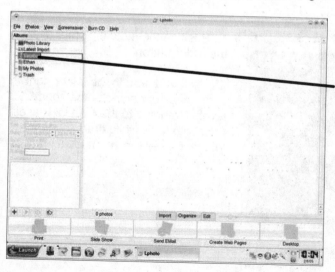

1. Press Ctrl+N on your keyboard. A new album will be created and you will be prompted to give it a name.

2. Type a name for your folder. It's a good idea to give it a descriptive name.

3. Press the Enter key and, the album will now be named.

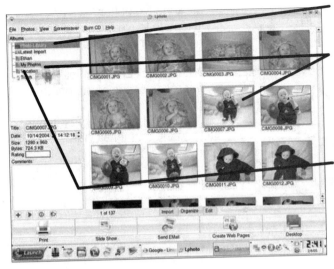

4.  Click on Photo Library to return to the photo library.

5.  Click and drag the photos you would like to add to an album. When you are over the album name, it will be highlighted, indicating that when you release the mouse button, the photo will be added to that album.

6.  Click on any album name to view its contents.

## Scaling Images

You can adjust the size of the thumbnails that appear in the window by clicking and dragging on a slider. It doesn't only work on thumbnails, as it can also be used when you have a picture open for editing. This tool is a great way to quickly zoom in and out of images.

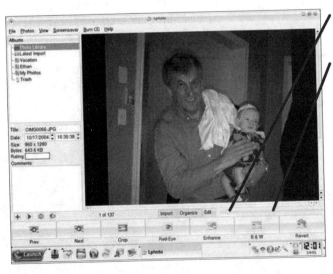

1.  Position the mouse pointer over the slider button.

2.  Click and drag to the left or right to increase or decrease the zoom level. Dragging to the right increases the zoom level while dragging to the left decreases the zoom level.

## Changing Photo Information

Typically, when you import photos from a digital camera, the photos are given a generic name and number. The problem with this is that the name associated with the photo really doesn't tell you anything about it. By changing the information of a photo, you'll make it easier to find and sort them later. You can even rate your photos so that you can later view them by their rating.

1. Click or double-click on any photo. You'll be able to edit a variety of information about your photo.

2. Type a name for your photograph.

3. Click the up or down arrows to adust the time and date.

4. Click in the Rating box to add a star rating to your photo. Keep clicking to the right to add more stars. Clicking on a star after it is there will remove it.

5. Type any comments that you would like to add about your photo.

*You can add photos to your library at any time by using the keyboard. Press Ctrl+O to bring up the Open dialog box from which you can select photos to import into the library.*

## Sorting Photos

The beauty of digital photos is that you can take as many photos as you like without having to develop them, which typically means that you'll have hundreds to thousands of photos. This can prove to be a problem when trying to find a particular image. Lphoto gives you several options for sorting your images to make them easier to find.

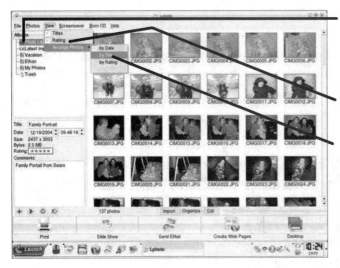

1. Click on the album that you would like to sort. Alternatively you can click on the Photo Library to sort all of your pictures.

2. Click View | Arrange Photos. A submenu will appear.

3. Click on the desired option. They include by Date, by Title and by Rating. The photos will now be sorted by the method you selected.

## Creating Slide Shows

Lphoto allows you to display your images as a full-screen slide show and gives you some control over how the slide shows are displayed.

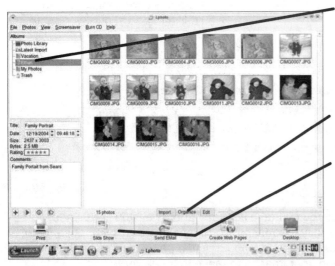

1. Click on the name of the album that contains the pictures you would like to view in a slide show. Alternatively you could click on the Photo Library to include all of your pictures in a slide show.

2. Click on the Organize tab if it is not already selected.

3. Click the Slide Show button. A dialog box will appear where you can set certain options for the show.

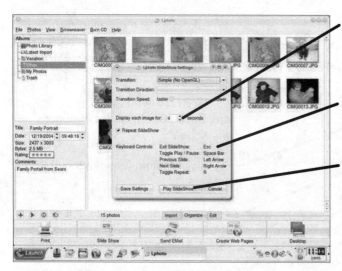

4. Click the up and down arrows to adjust the length of time each image is displayed before the next one appears.

5. Take note of the keyboard commands for controlling your slide show.

6. Click on the Play SlideShow... button. The slide show will begin to play.

7. Press the Esc key on the keyboard to end the slide show.

## E-Mailing Photos

One of the most convenient ways of sharing your photos with others is by e-mail  The only problem with e-mail is that your are typically limited to the size of a file you can attach to your message.  Lphoto solves this problem by allowing you to resize your pictures to make them e-mailable before they are sent.

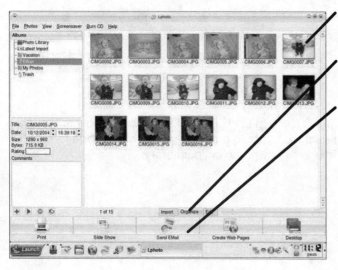

1. Click on the photo that you would like to e-mail.  It will be highlighted.

2. Click the Organize tab if it is not already selected.

3. Click the Send EMail button.  A dialog box will appear where you can adjust the image file size.

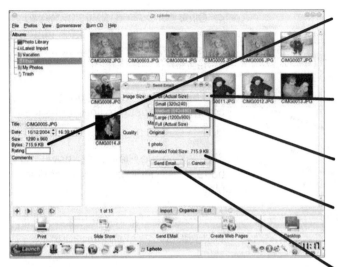

4. Take note of the size of the picture. If it is greater than 2000 KB proceed to Step 5 and 6 to resize it. Otherwise jump to Step 7.

5. Click on the Image Size drop-down menu. A list of options will appear.

6. Click Medium to make the size smaller.

7. Note the new file size. If it is still larger then 2000 KB repeat Steps 5 and 6, selecting a smaller option.

8. Click Send E-Mail... The E-Mail Client will launch and the photo that you selected will be loaded as an attachment to a message. You can then proceed to type in your e-mail message, select a recipient and send the e-mail.

*If you haven't already configured the E-Mail Client, you'll be prompted to do so when you attempt to send a picture. Instructions on doing this can be found in the chapter entitled "E-Mail."*

## Adding Photos to the Desktop

In the chapter entitled "Personalizing & Customizing Linspire" you learned how to use an image as the background for your desktop. Lphoto provides you with a method to instantly change the background image to any photo in your library.

1.  Click on the photo that you would like to use as your background image.

2.  Click the Organize tab if it is not already selected.

3.  Click the Desktop button.  The photo you selected will now be your desktop background image.

## Fixing Photos

Lphoto provides you with a variety of different tools to help you touch up your photos.  All of these effects can be applied at the touch of a button.

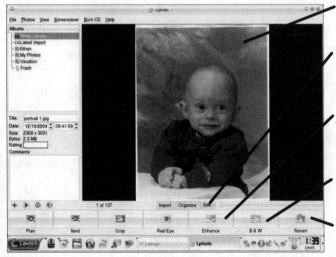

1.  Double-click on the photo that you would like to edit.

2.  Click on the Edit tab.  You'll be presented with different editing options.

3.  Click on the Enhance button. Lphoto will automatically adjust the colors and brightness of the image.

4.  Click the B & W button to convert your image to black and white.

5.  Click the Revert button at any time to bring your image back to its original state.

## Importing Photos from a Digital Camera

If there is an easier way than using Lphoto to get pictures from your digital camera onto your computer, I certainly haven't found it.  With a few clicks of the mouse button, all of your photos will be downloaded into the program.

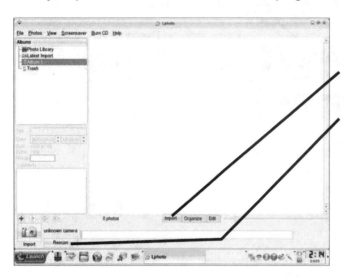

1.  Connect your digital camera to the computer and turn it on.

2.  Click the Import tab.  You will now see options for importing photos.

3.  Click the Rescan button.  Lphoto will scan your computer looking for any digital cameras that are attached and turned on.

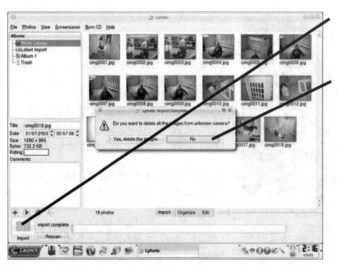

4.  Click the Import button.  All of the photos on the digital camera will be imported to the Photo Library.

5.  Click on the desired button in the dialog box that appears.  Clicking the "Yes, delete the images." button, will delete the images on the digital camera, while clicking the "No" button will leave them on the camera.

# Connecting to the Internet

There's a good likelihood that the bulk of the time that you spend on your computer will be used surfing the web, e-mailing, chatting or downloading files. To get access to the wonderful world of the Internet you will have to configure your connection. In some cases, this is simply a matter or plugging in your network cable and you are off and running. In other cases you'll need to configure your computer for use with an Internet Service Provider (ISP). Whether you are using a dial-up modem, a cable modem or some other broadband connection, Linspire makes it relatively easy to connect to the Internet.

There are also a variety of troubleshooting tools you can use should you come across some issues while trying to connect to the Internet. Once you are connected, you'll be able to explore the features described in the following chapters including surfing the web, e-mailing, and chatting.

In this chapter we'll cover:

- Setting up a dial-up connection
- Configuring a broadband connection
- Troubleshooting connection issues

**9**

# Selecting an Internet Service Provider

If you do not already have an ISP, Linspire gives you a range of choices that you can use to sign up with, directly from your computer. The beauty of using one of these providers is that Linspire has done their homework and selected those ISPs that work well in a Linux environment.

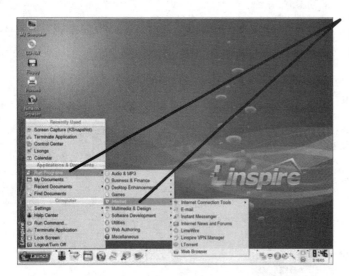

1. Click Launch | Run Programs | Internet. A submenu of Internet options will appear.

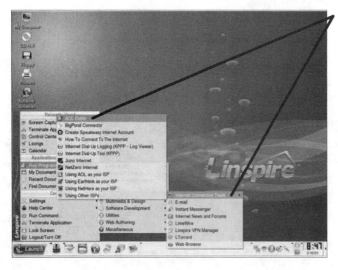

2. Click Internet Connection Tools and then click on one of the desired ISPs. There will be several to choose from. Depending on the ISP you select, what happens next will differ. Typically, though, a wizard will appear taking you step-by-step through the process of creating an account with that ISP. Simply follow the on-screen instruction for creating an account.

# Configuring a Dial-Up Connection

If you are using a dial-up connection, you'll need to obtain some information from your ISP before you can properly setup your Internet connection. This information includes the access phone number(s) of your provider, your user name and your password. There is one other essential component that you'll need to in order to use a dial up connection - a modem! It may seem obvious, but not all Linspire computers come with a modem, so ensure that you not only have a modem, but that the phone line is connected.

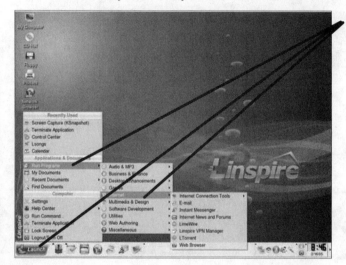

1. Click Launch | Run Programs | Internet. A submenu of Internet options will appear.

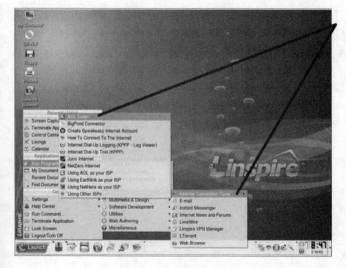

2. Click Internet Connection Tools | Internet Dial-Up Tool. The Internet Dial-Up Tool dialog box will appear.

*You may be asking yourself, "What if I don't have an ISP?" You can sign up with an ISP directly from your computer. This was covered earlier in the section entitled "Selecting an ISP."*

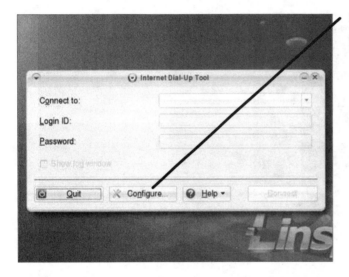

3. Click on the Configure... button. A dialog box will appear where you can configure your connection.

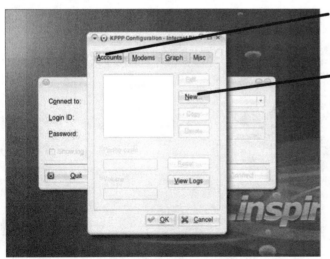

4. Click on the Accounts tab if it is not already selected. You can now create a new account.

5. Click the New... button. The New Account dialog box will open where you will create a name and add the phone number for your connection.

6.  Type a name for your connection. You can give it any name, but typically this would be the name of your ISP, e.g. AOL, Earthlink, Net Zero, etc.

7.  Click on the Add button. You will now be able to add the access phone number that was provided from your ISP.

8.  Type the number and click OK. The access number will be added.

9.  Repeat Steps 9 - 10 if there are any other access numbers that your ISP Provided you with.

10.  Click OK. The account will now be configured. You must now configure your modem.

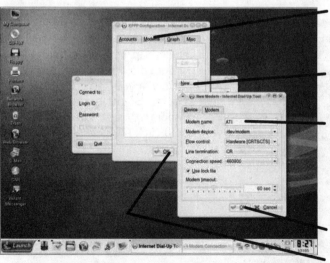

11.  Click on the Modems tab. If your modem appears in the list then you can skip to the next section.

12.  Click New. You will now be able to add your modem to the list.

13.  Type a name for your modem and use any of the drop-down menus to change the configuration of your modem if needed. You can also click the Modem tab to further configure your modem if necessary.

14.  Click OK. Your modem is set up.

15.  Click OK to close the Configuration dialog box. You will now be taken back to the Internet Dial-Up Tool dialog box which, you can leave open if you plan on connecting to the Internet now, or you can close it by clicking the Quit button.

## Connecting with a Dial-Up Modem

Once you have your connection and modem configured, dialing up is simply a matter of entering your user name and password.

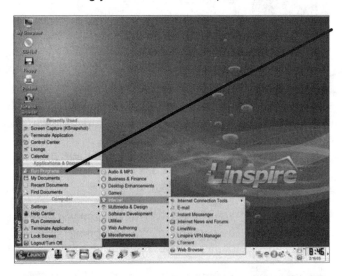

1. Click Launch | Run Programs | Internet. A submenu of Internet options will appear.

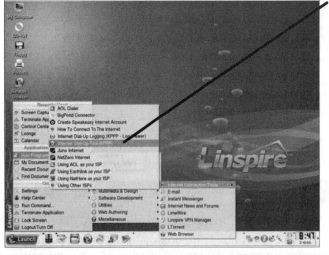

2. Click Internet Connection Tools | Internet Dial-Up Tool. The Internet Dial-Up Tool dialog box will appear. Alternatively, if you see a dialer for your specific ISP, select that instead. For example, if you are using AOL, you would click AOL dialer.

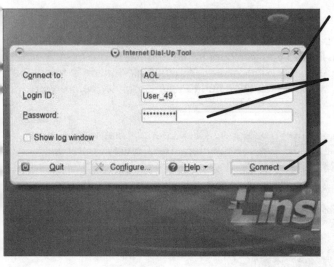

3.  Select your ISP from the drop-down list if you have more than one configured.

4.  Type your Login ID (also known as your User ID) and password in the fields provided.

5.  Click Connect.  Your modem will now dial up your ISP and connect you to the Internet. The dialog box will remain open, but it can be minimized.  Once connected you can use any Internet-related feature like instant messaging, web browsing or e-mail.

# Disconnecting the Internet Connection

Once you're done using the Internet, it's a good idea to disconnect as it will free up your phone line and you won't use up any more of your hours, if your ISP limits your usage.

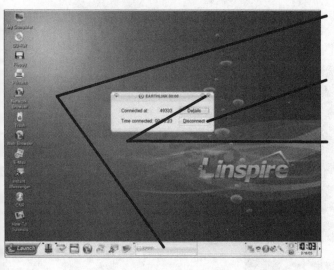

1.  Click on the button in the Taskbar that represents your connection.  A dialog box will appear.

2.  Click the Disconnect button.  You will be disconnected from the Internet.

3.  Click the Close button to close the dialog box.

# Connecting with DSL

If you have a DSL connection, you'll need your account name and password from your ISP before you can properly configure your connection. With that information in hand, the rest is a breeze - just make sure your cable is connected to your computer before you begin.

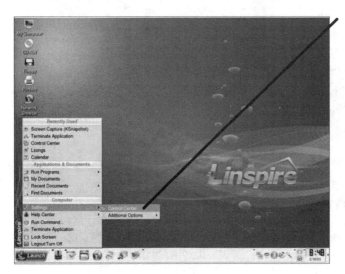

1. Click Launch | Settings | Control Center. The Control Center will open.

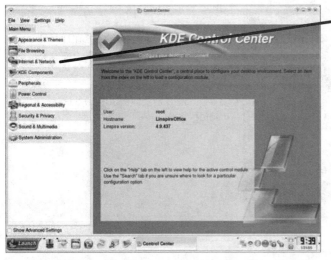

2. Click the Internet & Network link. The screen will change to give you Internet options.

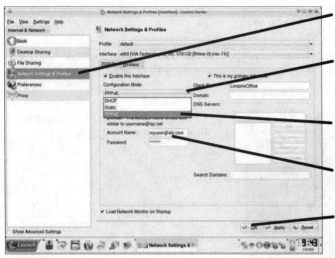

3.  Click on the Network Settings & Profiles link.

4.  Click on the Configuration Mode drop-down.  A list of options will appear.

5.  Click on PPPoE.  It will now be selected.

6.  Type in your account name and password in the fields provided.

7.  Click OK.  A dialog box will appear, confirming that you would like to make those changes.

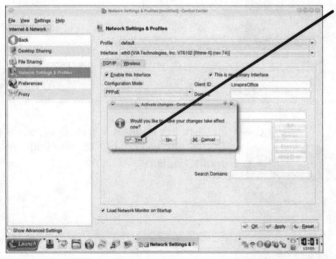

8.  Click the Yes button.  A connection to the Internet will be made and you'll be able to use all of the Internet-related tools.

# Troubleshooting a Cable Modem

If you are using a cable modem, Linspire should automatically recognize your connection and should require no further setup. If for some reason you cannot connect to the Internet, try the following steps before contacting support.

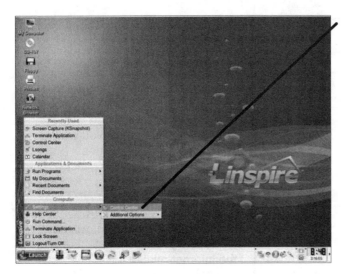

1. Click Launch | Settings | Control Center. The Control Center will open.

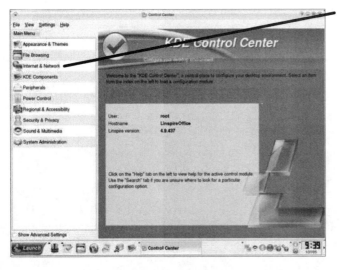

2. Click the Internet & Network link. The screen will change to give you Internet options.

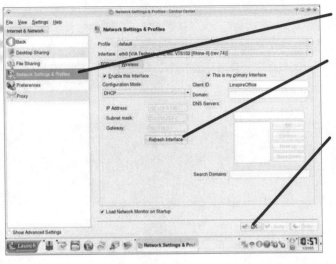

3. Click on the Network Settings & Profiles link.

4. Click the Refresh Interface button. Linspire will refresh your connection in an attempt to get your connection to work properly.

5. Click the OK button. A dialog box will open confirming whether or not you would like to accept the changes you've made.

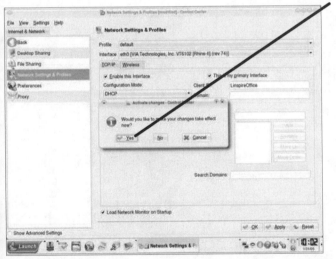

6. Click the Yes button. You can now try any of your Internet applications to see if your connection works.

# Installing Programs

# 10

The good folks at Linspire should moonlight as futurists. If you're not familiar with the term, a futurist is simply someone who predicts the future. Several years ago they came up with an idea of how software programs should be distributed, and their method is now becoming increasingly popular amongst many software vendors. Imagine being able to walk into your favorite computer software store, grab any program off the shelf, walk out of the store and not have to pay a thing. That's pretty much how it works with Linspire. Rather than having to go out and purchase programs, they have a subscription service that allows you to download as much software as you want while you are a member. Linspire's version of this is called CNR and as a subscriber you get access to thousands of dollars worth of software included in your subscription fee.

While CNR is by far the easiest and most recommended way to install programs on your Linspire computer, it is not the only method. Advanced users have the option of downloading programs off the web or installing from disk or CD.

In this chapter we'll cover:

- Signing up for a CNR subscription
- Navigating and using CNR
- Uninstalling and updating programs

# Creating a CNR Subscription

In order to take advantage of this revolutionary feature, you must have a subscription to the CNR Service. When you first started your Linspire computer, you may have seen a window open where you could sign up for a 15-day trial membership. Here we will walk you through obtaining your trial membership so you can test CNR before you make the commitment to buy. I can almost guarantee that after only a few minutes on CNR, you'll want to make the move to the yearly membership. The process of signing up is quite simple, and within minutes you'll be downloading programs to your heart's content. It actually takes two steps. The first is to register for a free account, which gets you access to security updates free of charge and the second is to acquire the subscription.

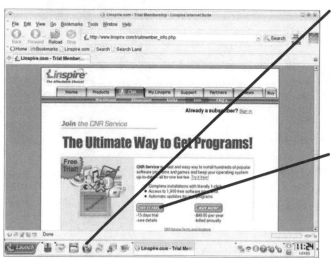

1. Click on the Web Browser. The Web Browser will launch and by default it should open to a page where you can sign up for your CNR subscription. If the trial membership page doesn't appear, type www.linspire.com/freetrial in the Location bar of the browser.

2. Click on the TRY IT FREE button. You will now be prompted to enter your billing information. Keep in mind that if you do not cancel your subscription within the trial period, you will be automatically billed for the one year subscription.

*Because CNR is an ever-evolving web-based program, some of the screens may be updated over time. The following instructions were accurate at the time of publication.*

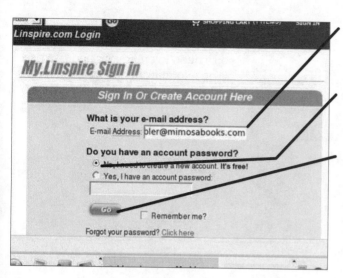

3. Type in your e-mail address. This will be your user name whenever accessing the Linspire web site.

4. Click the radio button beside No, I need to create a new account. It's free!

5. Click the Go button. You will now have to create and confirm a password.

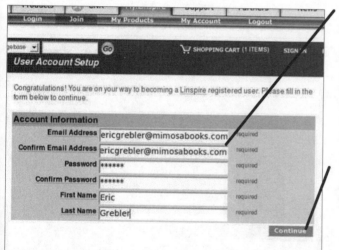

6. Type in the requested information into the fields provided. Here you are just being asked to confirm your e-mail address, create a password and enter your name. When you type and confirm you password it will appear as a series of stars so nobody looking over your shoulder will be able to steal your password.

7. Click the Continue button. A screen will appear where you will be prompted to create an address.

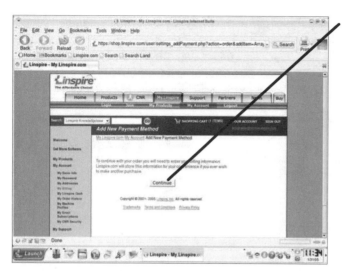

8. Click the Continue button to proceed to the next screens where you'll need to enter your address and billing information.

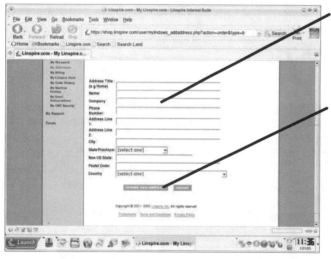

9. Type in all of the requested information. You can press the Tab key on the keyboard to move from one field to the other, or you can simple click on the desired field.

10. Click the create new address button. You will now be prompted to enter your credit card information.

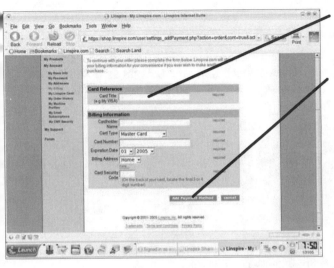

11. Type in the requested information into the appropriate fields.

12. Click the Add Payment Method button.

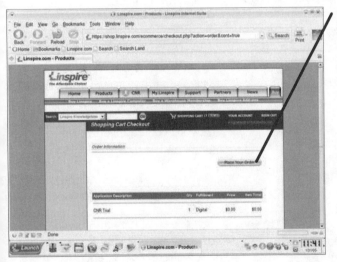

13. Click on the Place Your Order button to finalize your trial membership order. A screen will appear thanking you for your order. You will now be able to login to CNR with the e-mail address and password you supplied.

# Launching CNR

The CNR icon can be found on your desktop. Because you'll be using it so often, it may be a good idea to add the icon to your Quick Launch bar. Instructions on doing this are located in the "Personalizing and Customizing Linspire" chapter of the book.

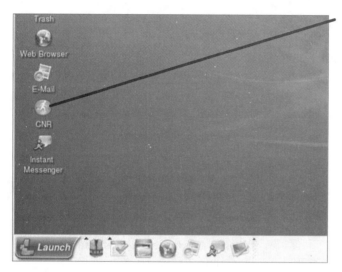

1. Double-click on the CNR icon. CNR will launch.

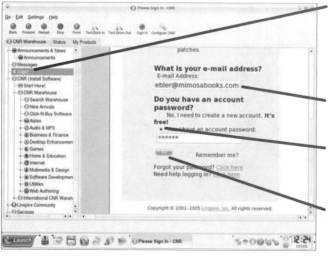

2. Click on the Login link on the left side of the screen. You will now need to enter the e-mail address and password you supplied when registering.

3. Type in your e-mail address and password in the fields provided.

4. Click the radio button beside, "Yes, I have an account password:" if it is not already selected.

5. Click Go. You are now signed in and ready to explore the world of CNR.

# Finding Programs

There are a variety of ways in which you can search for software in CNR. CNR has a web-style search engine that allows you to conduct searches by certain keywords. Those keywords can be based on the functionality of the software, the name of the manufacturer or the title of the application. Alternatively, if you're the type of person who prefers to walk the aisles while shopping to look for ideas, you can browse for different software by category.

## Searching

If you're hunting for a particular piece of software, you can run a web-style search in CNR and you'll be provided with all the results that match your criteria. You don't necessarily have to know the name of the program you are looking for, as you can just type in a keyword. For example, if you were looking for a photo manipulation tool, you could type in "photo" as the search term or, if you were looking for a piece of software from a particular vendor, let's say Adobe, you could simply type "Adobe" into the search box. After you've conducted your search, you can determine how you want the results displayed.

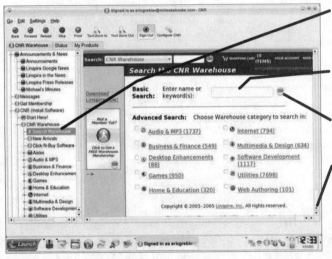

1. Click on the Search Warehouse link. You will now be able to conduct a search.

2. Type in the desired keyword for your search into the field.

3. Click Go. The results of your search will be displayed.

4. Click the scroll buttons to review your search. You can now either repeat Steps 1 - 3 to conduct another search or you can jump to the section entitled "Installing Programs with CNR" on the following pages.

# Browsing by Category

Like most men, I can spend hours just roaming the aisles of my local Home Depot, admiring the goods and getting an idea of what type of things I need for around the house. If you too like to browse for ideas, then you'll enjoy shopping the aisles of CNR. The programs in CNR are divided into a variety of categories that you can browse.

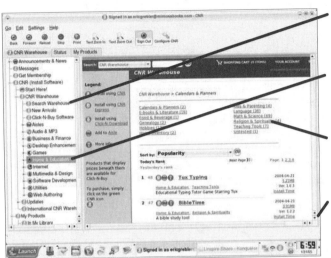

1. Click on the Search Warehouse link. You will now see several general categories of software.

2. Click on the desired category. The screen will change and you will see a list of subcategories.

3. Click on the desired subcategory. All of the programs that fall under that category will be displayed.

4. Use the scroll buttons to browse through the different software applications that have been found.

*Beside each of the categories you may have noticed a number in brackets. This number represents the number of programs that fall under that category.*

# Browsing by Aisle

Think of an aisle as a group of software that falls under a specific purpose or task rather then just a category. For example, if you're a graphic designer, you're probably looking for programs that might span a variety of categories including photo editing, page layout, art and vector programs. Linspire has a wide range of aisles that contain groups of programs designed for specific users or uses. Some examples of aisles include student aisles, developer aisles, kids aisles, web aisles and many more. Not only can you browse through the different aisles, but you can also create your own. The Linspire community becomes evident when working with aisles as every aisle you create can potentially be viewed by other members of the community.

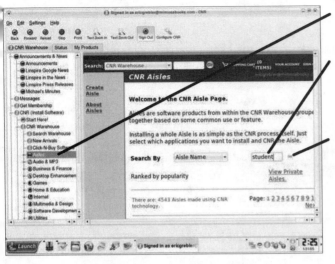

1. Click on the Aisles link on the left side of the screen.

2. Type a name for the type of aisle your looking for. Some examples of search terms would be student, kids, design or web.

3. Click the Go button. All of the results that match your search will be displayed.

Linspire gives you the ability to change the size of the text in CNR without adjusting your monitor's resolution. Simply click the Text Zoom In or Out buttons on the toolbar.

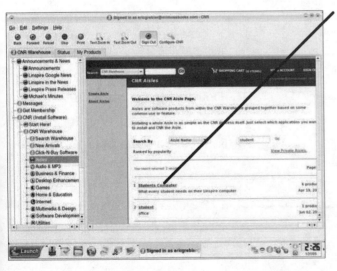

4. Click on the desired result to see all of the programs that fall within that aisle. A list of all the programs that fall within that aisle will appear. When you are ready to download and install a program, proceed to the section entitled "Installing Programs with CNR."

# Creating Aisles

You always have the ability to create your own aisles in Linspire. Whether you've got a great idea for an aisle that you'd like to share or if you'd just like to group some programs for your own use, creating an aisle is a breeze.

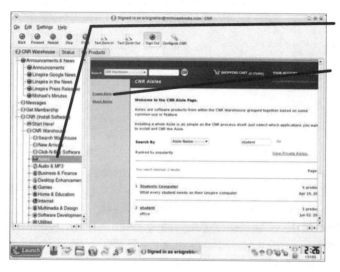

1. Click on the Aisles link on the left side of the page.

2. Click the Create Aisle link. You will now be prompted to add information about your link.

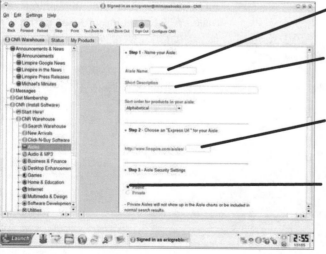

3. Type a name for your Aisle in the field provided.

4. Type a short description that tells about the type of programs that will be found in your aisle.

5. Type in a name for an express URL. This will provide you quick access to your aisle.

6. Click the radio button to make your aisle Public or Private.

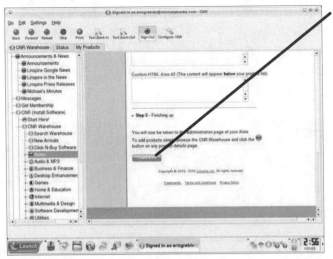

7. Scroll to the bottom of the page and click the Create Aisle button. Your aisle will be created and you can now add programs to that aisle. Keep in mind that you can create as many aisles as you'd like.

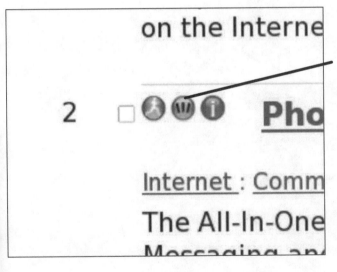

8. Search for programs using any of the search methods.

9. Click the Add to Aisle button beside any of the programs that you would like to add to an aisle. It is the orange button with three lines in it.

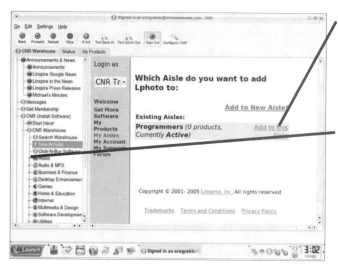

10.  Click on the Add to this Aisle link beside the aisle that you would like to add this program to.  Alternatively you can click the Add to New Aisle link if you want to create a new aisle for this program.

11.  Click on the + beside Aisles in the left panel of the screen.  The area under Aisles will expand.

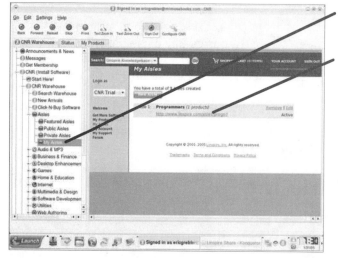

12.  Click the My Aisles Link.  A list of all your aisles will appear.

13.  Click on the link under the desired aisle to view its contents.

# Installing Programs with CNR

Now that you know how to find programs, it's time to start installing them. It's incredibly easy to add programs to your Linspire computer using CNR.

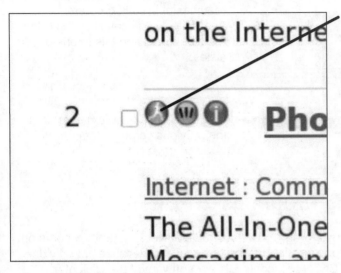

1. Click on the CNR logo beside the name of the program you want to load. The CNR logo is green and has a white image of a man running in it. The program will be downloaded and installed to your computer. Take note of the category that the program falls under as this is where you will find it on the Launch menu.

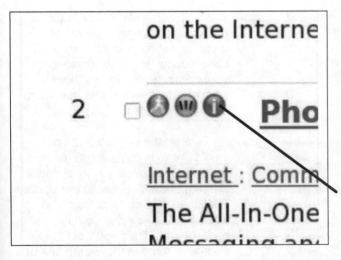

## Getting Program Information

You may have noticed during your search for programs that there was a little blue icon beside the names of certain programs. You can use this button to get additional information on the programs in CNR.

1. Click on the blue button that appears beside a program name. The screen will now change to provide you with information on that program.

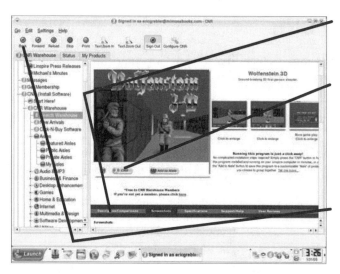

2. Click on any of the Description/Comparison links to get even more information on the title.

3. Click the CNR button if you are ready to install this program. Alternatively you can click the Add to Aisle button to add this to one of your aisles.

or

3. Click the Back button to return to the previous screen.

# Updating and Removing Programs

Don't you just hate it when you buy a program and a couple of weeks later they come out with a new version?  You'll have one less worry when using CNR, because not only do you not have to pay for updates, CNR can update all your software at the click of a button.  CNR  also keeps tracks of all the programs you've installed, on any computer, so it knows exactly what you have and what needs to be updated.

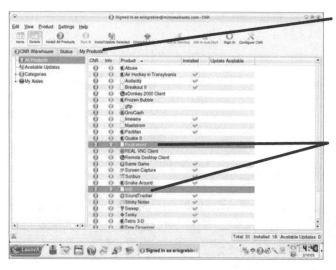

1. Click on the My Products tab at the top of the page.  You will be taken to a screen that shows all of the products you have installed on your computer as well as those where an installation was attempted but not completed.

2. Click on the product that you would like to update, install  or remove.  If an update is available, a check mark will appear in the Update Available  column.  You can hold down the Ctrl key and click on multiple products if you would like update or remove more than one at a time.

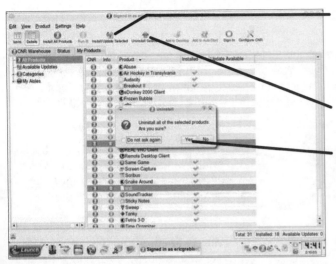

3. Click the Install/Update Selected button. The highlighted programs will be updated.

or

3. Click on the Uninstall Selected button.

4. If you selected Uninstall, click Yes at the dialog box to confirm that you would like to uninstall the selected programs. The program will be removed from your system.

## Managing Your CNR Account

You can view the status of your account, change passwords, and adjust your address and billing information from the My Account section of CNR.

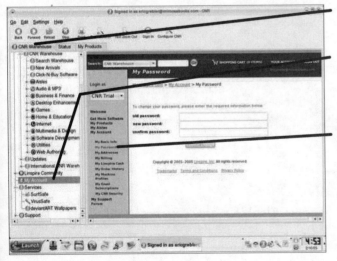

1. Click on the CNR Warehouse tab if it is not already selected.

2. Click on the My Account option. The main page of the My Account window will appear, showing you the current status of your subscriptions.

3. Click on any of the links to move to the desired screen. Once you are there you can follow the on-screen directions for changing any of the information. For example, if you clicked on the My Password link, there will be instructions on changing your password.

# Click-N-Buy

You may have noticed while browsing the aisles of CNR that some programs had a price labeled underneath their listing. While most programs in the CNR Warehouse come free with your subscription, there are other premium packages that need to be paid for if installed. As a CNR member you get a significant discount off the retail price of these products.

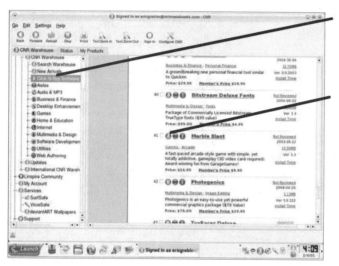

1. Click on the Click-N-Buy option on the left side of the window. A list of different software packages available for purchase will appear.

2. Click on the green CNR button beside the program that you would like to purchase. Your shopping cart summary screen will appear.

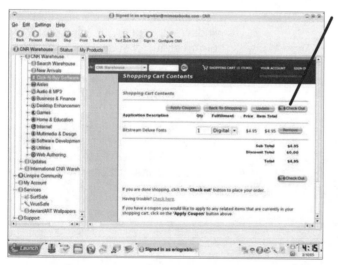

3. Click on the Check Out button. A screen confirming your credit card information will appear.

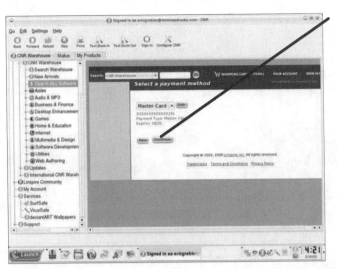

4. Click the Continue button if the credit card that you would like to use is listed. Otherwise, click the Add button to add a different credit card to use.

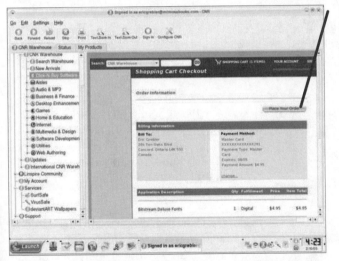

5. Click the Place Your Order button. The product that you purchased will now be downloaded to your machine.

*Linspire also gives you the option of purchasing services like virus protection and parental controls for web browsing. These features can be found by clicking the Services option.*

# Autostarting Programs

I love listening to the radio through Lsongs when I work on the computer. This program is so important to me that I have it start automatically when the Linspire operating system launches. You can do the same with any program.

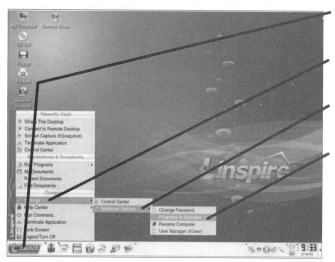

1. Click Launch. The Launch menu will appear.

2. Click Settings. A submenu will appear.

3. Click Additional Options. Another submenu will appear.

4. Click Programs to Autostart. A window will appear with all of the programs that are currently set to autostart.

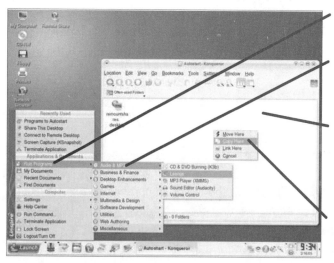

5. Click Launch | Run Programs. A list of categories will appear.

6. Click the category under which the program you would like to autostart falls.

7. Click and drag the program that you would like to autostart to the Autostart window. When you release the mouse button, a menu will appear.

8. Click Copy Here. A shortcut will appear in this window. This program will now start automatically whenever you start your computer.

# A Word on Word and Other Windows Software

A frequent question I get asked is, "Can I install Microsoft Word or other Microsoft Windows applications on my Linspire computer?" My typical response is, "Why would you want to?" Linspire provides you with thousands of programs at less than the price of one component of the Microsoft Office suite. In addition, the OpenOffice suite that comes with Linspire is highly compatible with Microsoft Office. Running Windows-based applications on any Linux operating system is like trying to fit a square peg into a round hole. It can be done but the results vary and can make your system unstable. If you still want to install a Windows application even after my little sermon, then you can CNR a program called Wine. Wine is a windows emulator that fools a Windows-based program into thinking it's running on Windows rather than Linux. Beware though, results may vary!

Any programs installed outside of CNR will not be supported by Linspire. In other words, install these programs at your own risk.

# Browsing the Internet

To quote the immortal words of Homer Simpson: "They have the Internet on computers now?" Of course they do, and really, is there anything that the Internet can't do? From finding recipes, to watching videos, to sharing pictures, to auctioning goods, to you name it, you can do and see just about anything on the Internet. Linspire comes with its own built-in Web Browser designed specifically for you to surf the Internet with ease.

You may be thinking to yourself, "What's the big deal about surfing the Net?, you can just type in an address and away you go." While that may be true, to optimize your time on the web, there are a variety of tools that can make your experience faster, more secure and certainly more convenient.

In this chapter we'll cover:

- Navigating with the Web Browser
- Accessing your favorite sites
- Cleaning the history list
- Customizing the Web Browser

# Launching the Web Browser

An icon for the Web Browser is located on the Quick Launch bar so you always have instant access to it.

1. Click the Web Browser icon on the Quick Launch bar. The Web Browser will launch and you can begin surfing the Internet. Alternatively you can double-click the Web Browser icon on the desktop or use the Launch menu to start the program.

# Navigating the Web Browser

The Web Browser provides you with a variety of different tools for getting around the Internet. From basic browsing to creating bookmarks, and link buttons, to tabbed browsing, navigating through the Internet has never been easier.

## Basic Browsing

Browsing the Internet is like looking through the pages of a book: you can move forward in your book, backwards, or you can jump to specific pages.

*When entering a URL into the Web Browser, you can save yourself a few keystrokes as you don't have to include the http:// before the address you'd like to visit.*

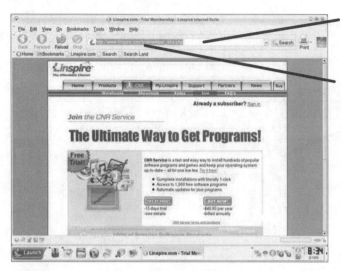

1. Double-click in the Location bar. The contents of the Location bar will be highlighted.

2. Type the address of the URL you'd like to visit.

3. Press Enter on your keyboard. You will be taken to the address you specified.

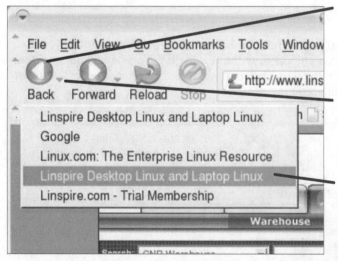

4. Click the Back button. You will be taken to the page you last visited. You can continue pressing the Back button to keep navigating back through the pages your visited.

5. Click the small gray arrow beside the Back button. A list of the previous pages you visited will be displayed.

6. Click on the desired page. This will allow you to jump back to a specific page you visited without having to continuously click the Back button.

*You can navigate back and forth through web pages by using your keyboard. Pressing the Alt key and the left arrow will move backwards and Alt and the right arrow moves forwards.*

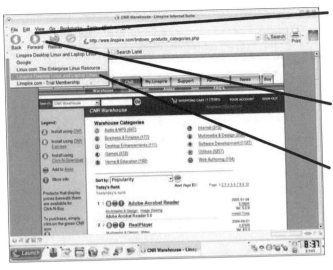

7. Click the Forward button. If you have pressed the Back button, the Forward button will be activated so you can move Forward to the page you had originally visited.

8. Click the gray down arrow to see a full list of the pages you can move forward to.

9. Click on the desired page. You will move forward to that page.

## Navigating with the History List

The Web Browser remembers the pages that you have visited, so if you want to quickly get back to a page you have visited you can use the history list. You can either view the entire history list, or you can begin typing a URL in the address bar and a list of sites that match the URL you are typing will appear.

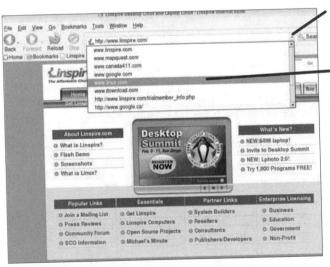

1. Click the down arrow at the end of the Location bar. A list of your recently visited sites will appear.

2. Click on the desired page that you would like to visit. You will be taken to that page.

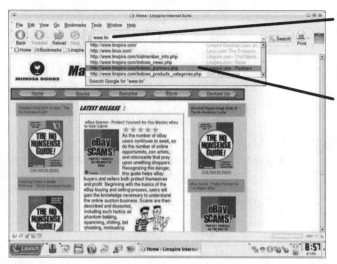

3. Begin typing a URL in the Location bar. As you type, web sites that your have previously visited that match will appear in the history list.

4. Click on the desired site you would like to visit.

## Tabbed Browsing

Typically when I'm on the Internet, I've got several windows open so that I can move back and forth to work on several sites. The problem with this is that it becomes difficult to keep track of which window contains which website. In addition, the more instances of a browser I have open, the more clutter on my computer. The solution to this is tab browsing. Tab browsing allows you to visit multiple web sites all within the same Web Browser window. You can jump through different sites by clicking on their respective tabs.

1. Click View. The View menu will appear.

2. Click Show/Hide. A submenu will appear.

3. Click Tab bar. The Tab bar will appear.

4.  Click the green + in the far left side of the Tab bar in order to create a new tab.  You can now navigate in this new tab as you would in any other web page.

5.  Repeat Step 4 to create any other tabs.

6.  Click on any tab to switch between different tabs.

7.  Click on the red "X" at the right side of the Tab bar to close a tab.

8.  Repeat Steps 1 - 3 to close the Tab bar.

## Using Bookmarks

There are just so many useful web sites out there that keeping track of them all could be a daunting task.  Rather then having to tax your brain's memory, you can use bookmarks. Just like the bookmark in the novel on your nightstand, bookmarks in the Web Browser allow you to quickly get to specific areas.

1.  Navigate to the page for which you would like to create a bookmark.

2.  Click Bookmarks from the menu bar.  The Bookmarks menu will appear.

3.  Click Bookmark This Page.  A bookmark will be created.

*Another way to create a bookmark is to use the keyboard. When you are at the page that you would like to bookmark, simply press Ctrl and the letter D on the keyboard.*

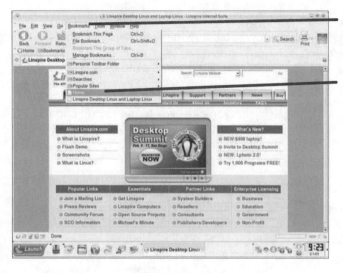

4. Click on Bookmarks in the menu bar. The Bookmarks menu will appear.

5. Click on the desired bookmark. You will be taken to that page.

## Using The Personal Toolbar

The Personal toolbar goes one step further than a bookmark. Rather than just remembering the location of a web site, a link will appear on the Personal toolbar that you can click on to instantly jump to a specific site. By default the Personal toolbar should be open, but if not, you can access it by following Step 1; otherwise proceed to Step 2. The Personal toolbar can be found under the Navigation toolbar.

1. Click View | Show/Hide | Personal Toolbar.

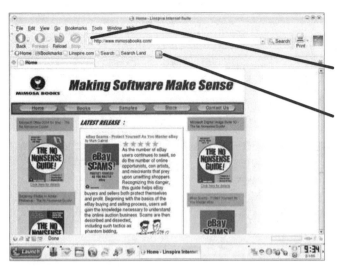

2.  Navigate to the page for which you would like to create a button.

3.  Position your mouse pointer over the logo at the left of the URL.

4.  Click and drag the logo until you are over the Personal toolbar.  As you drag the mouse pointer will change to a little piece of paper.

5.  Release the mouse button when you are over the Personal toolbar.  A link will appear on the toolbar that you can click to get to that page at any time.

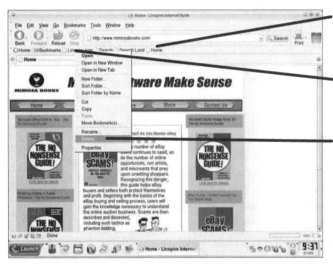

6.  Click on any link in the Personal toolbar.  You will be instantly taken to the page that the link represents.

7.  Right-click on any link that you would like to remove.  A menu will appear.

8.  Click Delete.  The link will be removed from of the Personal toolbar.

*When you create a link on the Personal toolbar, the link is given the default name of the current web site.  Links can be renamed by right-clicking on the link and clicking Rename.*

# Working in Web Pages

Once you've navigated to the pages you want to visit, you've got quite a few options. From downloading files and images, to jumping to other pages, to translating content, to finding text, there are a variety of tools that the Web Browser can help you with when you are working with web pages.

## Using Links

Within web pages you'll find links that will take you to different web sites or to different locations within the same web page. It used to be that all links were blue and underlined, but this standard has since changed. Typically, you'll know when you are over a link when the mouse pointer changes to a little hand.

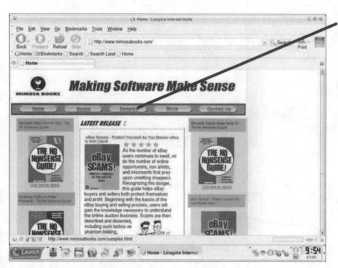

1. Position the mouse pointer over a link. The mouse pointer will change to a hand to indicate that you are over a link.

2. Click on the link. You will be taken to the page associated with that link.

*If you right-click on a link, you'll be provided with a variety of options. Among other things, you can open the link in a new tab or window, and you can bookmark the link or page.*

## Finding Text on a Page

This is one of the features that I use most often when web browsing. If you're on a page, particularly one with a lot of information displayed, you can use the Find command to look for and find a particular word or string of text.

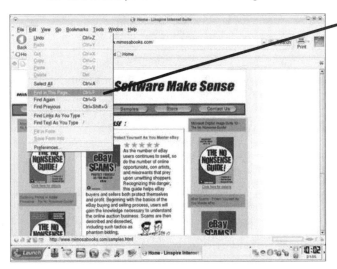

1.  Click Edit | Find in This Page... from the menu bar. The Find in this Page dialog box will appear, where you can enter the text that you would like to find.

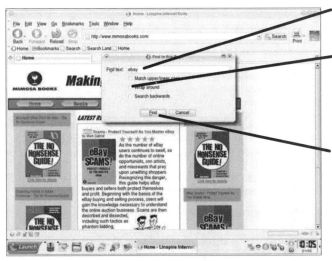

2.  Type the text string that you are looking for in the Find text: field.

3.  Click on any of the check boxes to select any of the options. You can choose to match a certain case, wrap around, or search backwards in the document rather than forwards.

4.  Click Find. The first instance of the word will be found and highlighted on the page.

5.  Repeat Step 4 to find other instances of the word(s) in the web page.

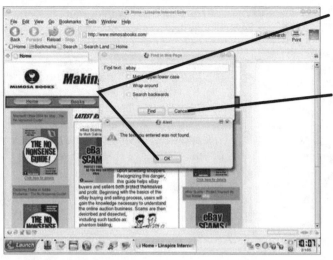

6.  Click OK when the Alert dialog box appears.  This indicates that the Web Browser can find no more instances of the text on the page.

7.  Click Cancel to close the Find in this Page dialog box.

# Downloading Files

The Internet is an amazing resource for finding all sorts of files.  What and where you download is up to you, but here's the process for handling downloads.

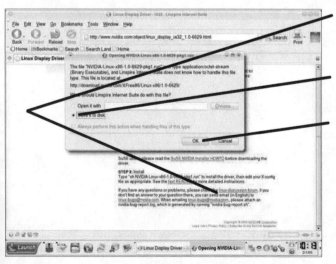

1.  Click on the link associated with the download.  A dialog box will appear.

2.  Click the radio button beside Save it to disk if it is not already selected.

3.  Click the OK button.  You will be prompted to specify a location to save the file on your computer.

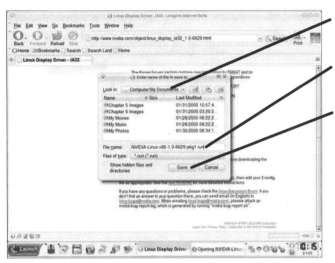

4. Navigate to the folder where you would like to save this file.

5. Type a file name if you want to replace the default name of the file.

6. Click Save. The download process will begin and a dialog box will appear showing you the progress of your download. The file will be saved to the location you have specified.

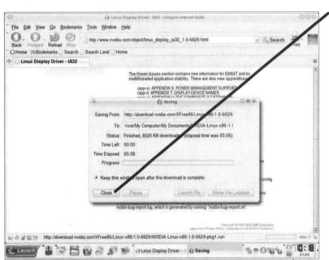

7. Click the Close button to close the Saving dialog box once the download is complete.

## Saving Images

Any image that you see on the web can be downloaded. Keep in mind that images that you save directly from a web page are low resolution. In other words, their image quality is low. Also keep in mind that many of the images you see on the Internet are copyrighted, so make sure you have permission before saving and using the images.

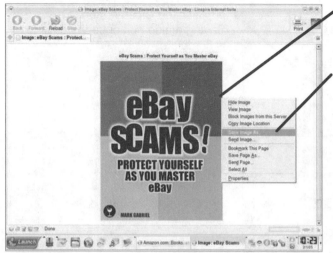

1.  Right-click on the image that you would like to download, and a menu will appear.

2.  Click Save Image As… A dialog box will appear where you can specify a location to save the image.

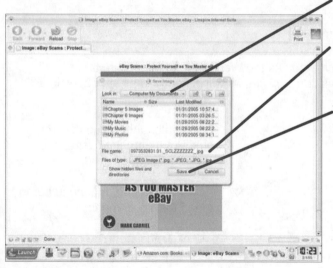

3.  Navigate to a folder where you would like to save the image.

4.  Type a new name for the image if you don't want to use the default name provided.

5.  Click Save. The download process will begin and a dialog box will appear showing you the process of your download. The file will be saved to the location you have specified.

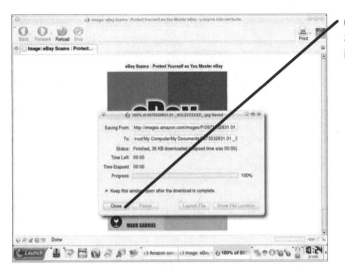

6. Click the Close button to close the Saving dialog box once the download is complete.

# Translating Pages

Put away your Spanish and French tapes as the Web Browser in Linspire takes advantage of Google's page translation services. It will instantly translate pages in a variety of different languages.

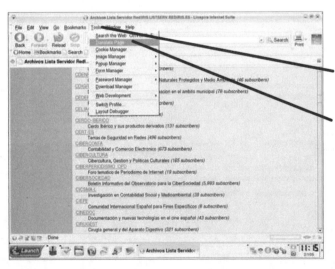

1. Navigate to the page that you would like to translate using one of the navigation methods.

2. Click Tools from the menu bar to expand the Tools menu.

3. Click Translate. The current page will be translated to English.

# Searching the Internet

There are a variety of different search web sites that allow you to filter through the web in search of your topic. The most prominent of these is Google, and the Web Browser incorporates the Google search engine into its Location bar. Beyond basic searches, you can use Linspire's Hot Words feature to immediately search on any word.

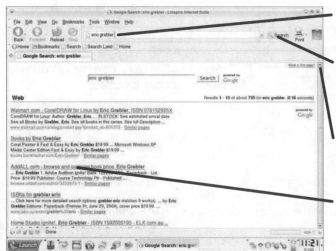

1. Type the term that you are searching for in the Location bar.

2. Click the Search button or simply click Enter on the keyboard. A list of the search results will be displayed in the window.

3. Scroll the different search results until you see one that matches what you were looking for.

4. Click on the desired link. You will be taken to that site.

*To conduct a search on an exact phrase, put a pair of quotations around the search text. Also keep in mind that the searches you conduct are not case-sensitive.*

## Hot Words Searching

The developers at Linspire have done it again. They've taken searching the web to an entirely different level by creating a revolutionary feature called Hot Words searches. This search functionality allows you to quickly search on any word you find on the Internet with just a click of the mouse button. Not only can you conduct regular searches with Hot Words, but you can search particular categories and even run grammar and spell checks on the term you've selected.

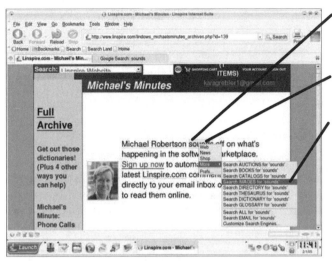

1. Position your mouse pointer over any word in a web page. The word will become highlighted.

2. Click on the highlighted word, and a menu will appear.

3. Click on the desired category of search you would like to conduct. If you click on the More category, you will see additional options. The results appear in a new tab. Your search options include:

- Web. This conducts a regular Google search on the highlighted term.

- News. This will search Google's news archive for the highlighted term.

- Shop. This will search Froogle.com's site for products for sale that match that term.

- Auctions. The eBay website will open and any auctions that match the highlighted term will be displayed.

- Books. A search on Amazon.com will be conducted on the highlighted term.

- Catalogs. A search on Google's Catalog search function will be conducted and results matching the word you highlighted will appear.

- Images. Any images that match the highlighted term will be displayed in Google's image search.

- Directory. A search will be conducted on the highlighted word using Google's directory service.

- Thesaurus. Selecting Thesaurus will launch Thesaurus.com and synonyms of the highlighted word will be displayed.

- Dictionary. Selecting this option will launch Dictionary.com and the definition of the highlighted word will be displayed.

- Glossary. Google will do a search of definitions of the highlighted word on the Internet.

# Managing the Web Browser

Everyone has different preferences when it comes to working on the computer, and using the Web Browser is no different.  You can configure and control how certain pages appear, manage how they are handled and determine how certain information is exchanged.

## Changing the Home Page

When you first start the Web Browser you are taken to a page that is called your Home page.  By default this page is the CNR trial membership sign up page, but it can be changed to any page you like.

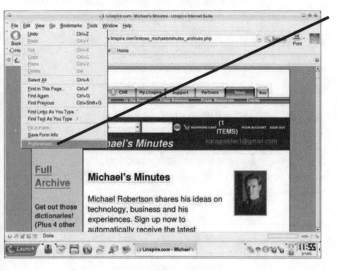

1.  Click Edit | Preferences…  The Preferences dialog box will open.

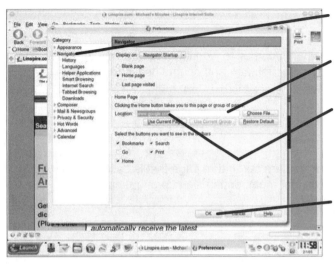

2. Click on the Navigator option if it is not already highlighted.

3. Double-click in the Location box. It will appear highlighted.

4. Type in the URL that you would like to use as your Home page. Alternatively you can click the Use Current Page button to use the current page as your Home page.

5. Click the OK button. Your changes will be accepted and your new Home page will be set.

## Clearing History and Cache

The Web Browser keeps track of all of the web sites that you have visited. You may have noticed that when you return to certain web sites, they remember who you are or they load up some preferences that you have set. In order for some pages to load faster and to remember data about you, a cache file with certain information and files on the sites you've visited is created. It's a good idea to occasionally clear this cache and also the history of the sites you've visited for the sake of privacy.

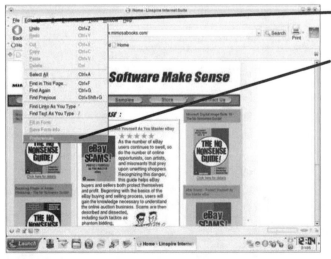

1. Click Edit. The Edit menu will appear.

2. Click Preferences. The Preferences dialog box will appear.

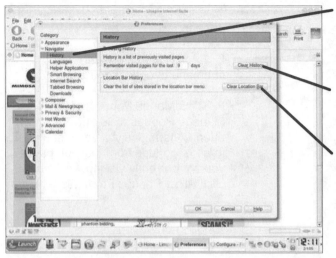

3.  Click on the History option.  It will be highlighted and you will see options for clearing your history of sites visited.

4.  Click the Clear History button to clear the history of the web pages you have visited.

5.  Click the Clear Location Bar button to clear the history of sites you've visited from the Location bar.

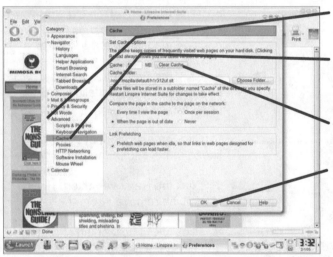

6.  Click the triangle beside Advanced to expand the options.

7.  Click on the Cache option.  A variety of cache configuration settings will appear.

8.  Click the Clear Cache button.  All the files in the cache will be deleted.

9.  Click the OK button to close the Preferences dialog box.

## Managing Popups

There's nothing more annoying when you're peacefully browsing the Internet, then to have a popup ad for the miracle medical cure of the week appear.  Popup ads are the Internet's equivalent to used car salesmen: annoying and inconsiderate.  Linspire's Web Browser is leading the war on popup ads as it automatically blocks them.  There are, however, occasions where legitimate web site uses popups.  You can let the Web Browser know from which sites it can accept popups.

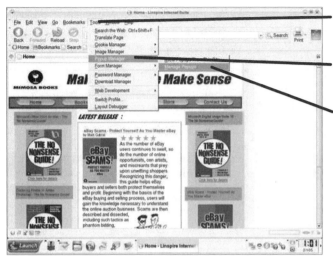

1.  Click Tools.  The Tools menu will appear.

2.  Click Popup Manager.  A submenu of options will appear.

3.  Click Mange Popups.  The Manage Popups dialog box will now open.  Alternatively, if you just want to allow popups from the web page you are currently visiting, you can click Allow Popups From this Site.

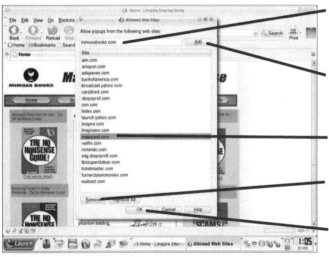

4.  Type the URL of the site that you would like to allow popups from.  You don't need to include the www.

5.  Click the Add button. The site will be added to the list of allowable popups.

6.  Click on any site that you would like to remove from the allowable list.

7.  Click the Remove button.  The site will be removed from the list.

8.  Click OK to accept the changes and close the dialog box.

## Changing Zoom Levels

Not all web pages appear the same.  Depending on how the fonts were created, they may be displayed in a manner that makes them difficult to see.  Rather then having to change your computers resolution in order to better see the text of a web page, you can simply use the built-in zoom controls.

*You can zoom in and out of a web page's text using the keyboard.  Hold down the Ctrl key and press the + key to zoom in or the  - key to zoom out.*

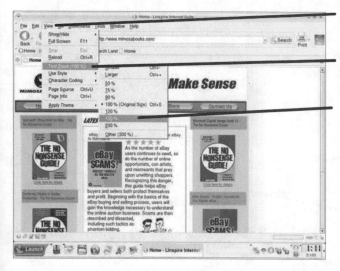

1.  Click View.  The View menu will appear.

2.  Click Text Zoom.  A submenu of different zoom options will appear.

3.  Click on the desired zoom level. If you selected anything under 100% the page will zoom out, while anything over 100% will zoom in.

## Showing and Hiding Toolbars

There are several toolbars that make up the Web Browser user interface.  Depending on you preferences, you can select which toolbars should appear on the screen and which should remain hidden.

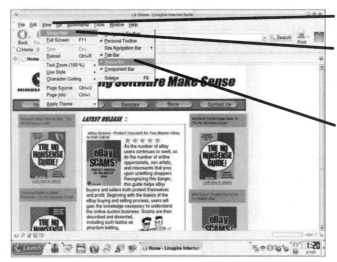

1.  Click View on the menu bar.

2.  Click Show/Hide to see a list of toolbars. Those toolbars that are currently open will have a check mark beside them.

3.  Click on the toolbar that you would like to show or hide. If it is currently open, it will close, otherwise the toolbar will appear.

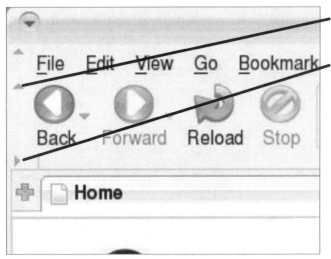

4.  Click on the gray up arrow beside a toolbar to temporarily hide it.

5.  Click on an gray arrow pointing right to expand a hidden toolbar.

# E-Mail

Do you remember the last time you sat down at your desk to handwrite a letter? If you're like most people, it's been at least a few years due to the popularity of e-mail. Why would you wait days to get your message to someone when you can beam it directly to your recipient over the Internet in seconds - no stamp required! As you may already know, e-mail can be your best friend or your worst enemy, depending on how you approach it.

The convenience of almost instantaneous communication can quickly be countered by the annoyance of spam (unsolicited e-mail), clutter and disorganization.

Linspire comes with its own e-mail software that you can use to send and receive messages. Before using this e-mail package you'll have to configure it so that it knows where to look to grab the mail that belongs to you. This information is typically available from your Internet Service Provider (ISP), so it's a good idea to get their contact information ready before proceeding with this chapter.

In this chapter we'll cover:

- Configuring the E-Mail Client
- Sending and receiving e-mails
- Organizing your messages

**12**

# New Account Setup

When you first launch the e-mail program you will be presented with the Account Wizard dialog box that will take you through the creation of your account. Because e-mail is so central to the work you do on your computer, it can be accessed directly from the Quick Launch bar.

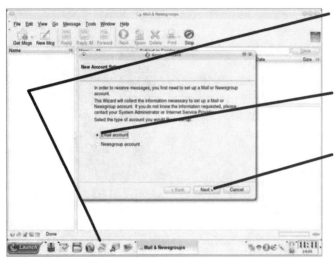

1. Click on the E-Mail Client button on the Quick Launch bar. The Account Wizard dialog box will appear.

2. Click the radio button beside Email account if it is not already selected.

3. Click the Next button to move to the next step of the process.

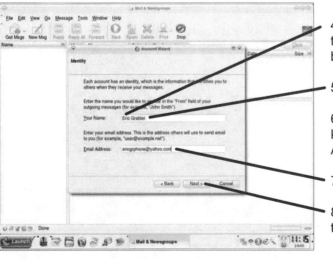

4. Click and drag across the existing text in the Your Name: field. It will become highlighted.

5. Type your name into the field.

6. Press the Tab key on your keyboard. The contents of the Email Address field will now be highlighted.

7. Type your e-mail address.

8. Click the Next button to move to the next step in the process.

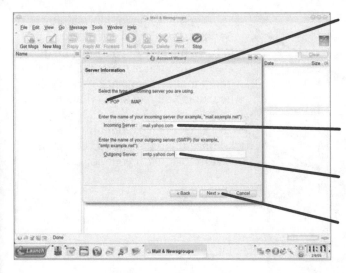

9.  Click the radio button beside the type of incoming server you are using.  This information, along with the information needed for Steps 10 and 11, can be obtained from your ISP.

10.  Type the name of your incoming server in the field.

11.  Type the name of your outgoing server in the field.

12.  Click Next to advance to the next stage in the process of setting up an e-mail account.

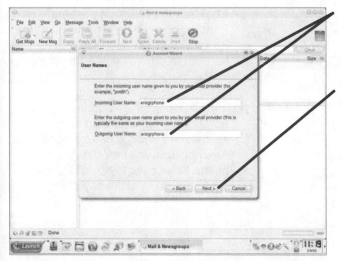

13.  Type the incoming and outgoing user name for your e-mail account.  Again, this information can be obtained from your ISP.

14.  Click on the Next button to move to the next step in the process.

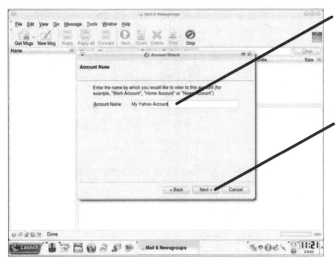

15.  Type a name for this account. Because the E-Mail Client allows you to have multiple accounts, it's a good idea to give the account a descriptive name that distinguishes it from other accounts you might be creating.

16.  Click the Next button.  You'll now be brought to the final screen of the wizard to confirm your settings.

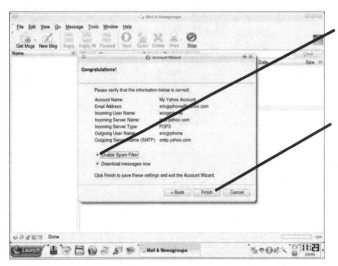

17.  Click the check box beside Enable Spam Filter.  This will turn the Spam Filter feature on for your account to prevent you from getting junk e-mail.

18.  Click the Finish button and your account will be created. You will now just have to enter your password. Alternatively, you can click the Back button to go back to any of the steps in the wizard to make any changes.

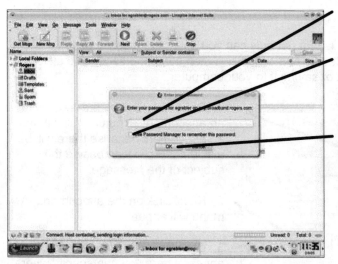

19.  Type in your password.  It will appear as a series of stars.

20.  Click the check box beside Use Password Manager to remember this password if you are the only one who has access to this computer.

21.  Click the OK button.  Existing messages on your e-mail server will be downloaded to your account.

# Receiving and Viewing E-mail

By default, the E-Mail Client will check the server every three minutes for e-mail. When new messages arrive, they will be placed in the Inbox folder for you to view.  New messages that have not been read appear in bold text.  The E-Mail Client window is split into a preview window where you can instantly read the contents of your messages. You can also choose to view  your messages in their own separate window.

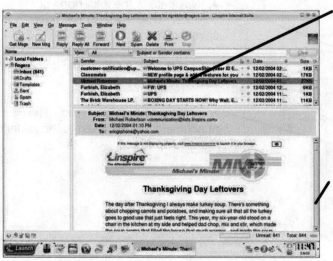

1.  Click on a message.  The contents of the message will appear in the preview window.  Alternatively you can double-click on a message, to open it in its own window.  When you are finished reading the message you can click the Close button in the top right corner of the window to close the message and return to your inbox.

2.  Scroll through the message to read its contents.

# Receiving Attachments

One of the key benefits of e-mail is that not only can you send and receive messages, but you can also send and receive files as attachments. When someone sends you a file, you have the option of opening it or saving it to your computer.

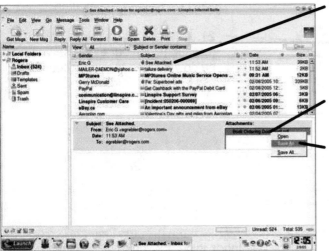

1. Click on an e-mail message with an attachment. You can tell if it has an attachment because there will be a little paperclip icon beside the subject of the message.

2. Right-click on the attachment. A menu will appear.

3. Click Save As... A dialog box will appear where you can specify where on your computer you would like the file saved. Alternatively you can click Open, which opens the file with the program that is associated with it.

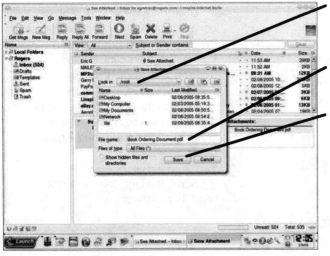

4. Navigate to the folder on your computer where you would like to save the file.

5. Give the file a new name if you so desire.

6. Click on the Save button. The attachment will be saved to the folder that you specified.

*Never under any circumstances open an attachment from someone you are unfamiliar with. The attachment could be a virus that could do damage to your computer.*

# Address Book

While using the Address Book is not essential, is does make things a whole lot easier. Storing your contacts means that you have instant access to them when sending messages. This is especially beneficial nowadays as there are so many free e-mail services, and people tend to have multiple e-mail addresses. Using the Address Book, you can add individual entries or you can create lists which allows you to send an e-mail to a group of people by only entering the name of the list.

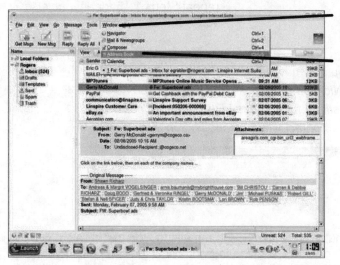

1. Click Window. The Window menu will appear.

2. Click Address Book. The Address Book program will launch.

*You can launch the Address Book at any time by pressing Ctrl+5 on your keyboard.*

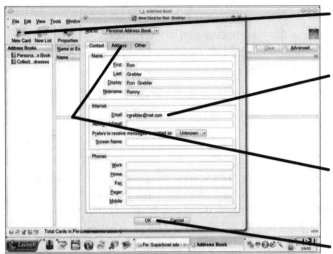

3. Click the New Card button. A window will appear where you can add someone to the Address Book.

4. Type the information of the person in the fields provided. None of the fields are mandatory but you should include their first and last name as well as their e-mail address.

5. Click on any of the other tabs to include additional information on the person you are adding to the Address Book.

6. Click OK. The person will be added to the Address Book. You can repeat Steps 1 - 5 for anyone else you would like to add.

*You may have noticed one of the fields called Nickname. A nickname can be used as a substitute for entering in the e-mail address of a contact when composing an e-mail.*

## Creating Lists

If you have a group of people that you routinely send e-mails to, you can create a list. Rather then having to type each person's address individually when composing your e-mail, you simply type in the name of the list and everyone on the list will receive that e-mail.

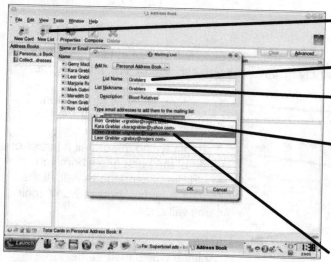

1. Click on the New List button. The Mailing List dialog box will appear.

2. Type a name for your list.

3. Type a nickname and description for the list if desired.

4. Click in the first empty line and begin typing the first or last name or nickname of the person you'd like to add to the list. All of the contacts in the Address Book that match the name you are typing will appear.

5. Click on the desired contact to add them to the list. Alternatively, if the person is not part of the Address Book, you can continue typing in their e-mail address until it's complete.

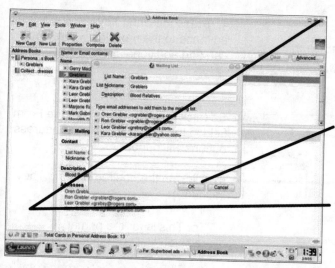

6. Repeat Steps 4 and 5 to add anyone else to your list.

7. Click OK. The list will now be created. The list will be added to the Address Book and can be accessed like any other address.

8. Click the Close button in the top right corner to exit the Address Book once finished.

*Double-click on any entry in the Address Book to open up a window where you can edit the address information.*

# Composing E-Mail

Sending messages to your friends, family and colleagues is a breeze in Linspire. Your messages can be formatted in a variety of ways and you can add files as attachments.

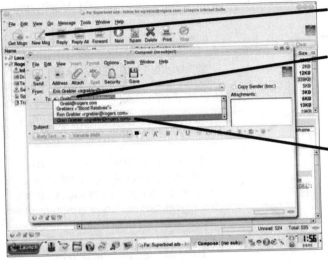

1. Click on the New Msg button. The Compose window will appear.

2. Begin typing the e-mail address or name of the person to whom you would like to send the e-mail. If the contact is in the Address Book, their name will appear.

3. Click on the desired recipient or continue typing their name.

4. Press the Enter key. You will advance to the next line where you can add additional recipients.

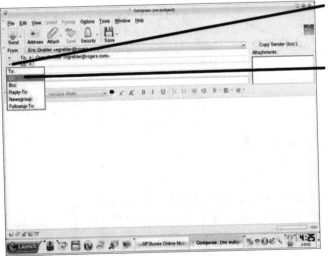

5. Click on the arrow under the From field in the next line. A list of address options will appear.

6. Click on the desired option. They include:

- To. This is for the primary recipients of your message.

- Cc. This stands for "carbon copy," which means that the recipient will receive a copy of the message and their name will be visible to everyone who received the message.

- Bcc. This stands for "blind carbon copy," which means that the recipient will receive a copy of the message, but their name will not be visible to anyone else who received the message.

- Reply-To. If you'd like any replies to go to different e-mail addresses, rather than the original addressees, use Reply-To.

- Newsgroup. This field is for posting your message to a newsgroup.

- Followup-To. This is used to redirect a newsgroup posting. All replies will go to this newsgroup rather than the original.

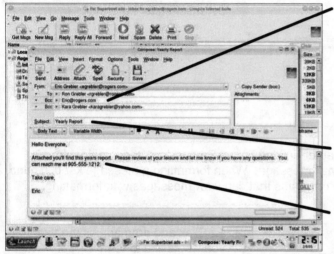

7. Type another e-mail address for the type or recipient you specified in Step 6.

8. Press the Enter key.

9. Repeat Steps 5 - 8 to add any other recipients.

10. Type a subject line for your e-mail. This is what recipients will see first, so make sure it is detailed.

11. Type your e-mail message in the window.

## Adding Attachments

You can add any files to send along with your messages as an attachment. You should keep in mind however that some mail servers limit the size of files that can be sent and received. If you use the general rule of thumb that your attachments should be no larger then 2 MB (2000 KB), you should be alright. Your ISP can let you know the maximum size of file you can send from your e-mail account.

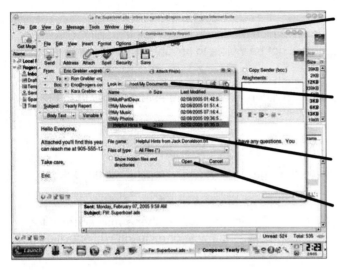

1.  Click the Attach button when composing your e-mail. The Attach File(s) dialog box will appear from which you can select a file.

2.  Navigate to the folder that contains the file that you would like to attach.

3.  Click on the file that you would like to attach. It will be highlighted.

4.  Click the Open button. The file will be attached to the e-mail.

5.  Repeat Steps 1 - 5 to add any additional files.

## Formatting Messages

If you've already reviewed the chapter entitled "Word Processing" then you're already familiar with how to format an e-mail message. When formatting a message keep in mind that not all e-mail recipients have programs that can view messages with formatting.

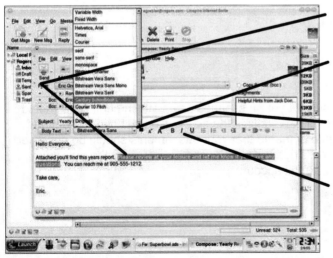

1.  Click and drag across the text that you would like to format.

2.  Click on the drop-down list to select a list of fonts and click on the desired font.

3.  Click on either of the font size buttons to increase or decrease the font size.

4.  Click on the Bold, Italics or Underline button to format the selected text with one of those features.

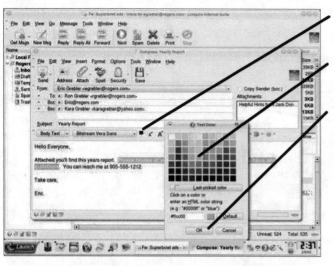

5. Click on the Font Color button. A dialog box will appear.

6. Click on the desired color. It will be selected.

7. Click the OK button. The color will be applied to your text.

## Spell Checking Messages

Because e-mail is primarily a text based method of communication, your words create a great impression of the type of person you are. To avoid being thought of as careless or lazy, your messages should be free of errors. The E-Mail Client helps you in this endeavor as it automatically checks your spelling as you type.

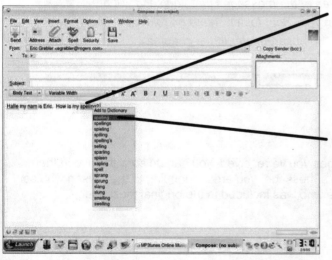

1. Position your mouse pointer over any word that has a red underline. The red underline indicates that the word cannot be found in the dictionary. The word will become highlighted and a list of alternatives will appear.

2. Click on the desired alternate word. The incorrect word will be replaced with the one that you have selected. Alternatively, you can click the Add to Dictionary option, if the word is spelled correctly but just not recognized by the dictionary. This is very common for proper nouns.

# Sending Messages

Once you have your e-mail message composed, sending it is just a matter of pressing the Send button.

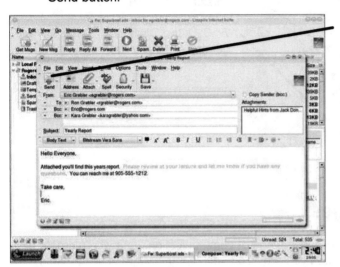

1. Click the Send button. The message will be sent to the recipients that you specified.

*Copies of the messages that you send will be kept in your Sent folder. More on folders will be covered later in the chapter.*

# Replying to Messages

If you'd like to respond to messages you've received, you can do so with ease in the E-Mail Client. When you reply to a message, you are responding to the person who sent it to you and potentially to anyone who was included in the original message.

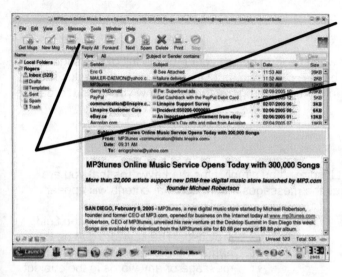

1.  Click on the message that you would like to reply to.  It will be highlighted.

2.  Click on the Reply or Reply All. Clicking Reply will send your message back to the original sender only while Reply All will send it to the original sender and anyone else who was copied on the message.

3.  Compose the message as you would any other.  The only difference is that the original message will be included in the body of the e-mail.

# Forwarding Messages

Forwarding messages works much in the same way as replying with the exception that you will have to specify who the message is forwarded to.  In addition, unlike when replying, any attachments to the original message will also be sent.

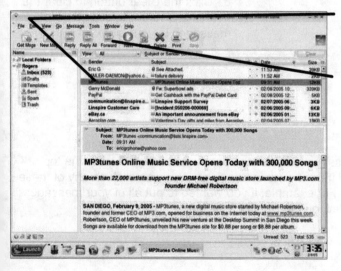

1.  Click on the message that you would like to forward.  It will be highlighted.

2.  Click on the Forward button.

3.  Compose the message as you would any other. You will have to specify recipients for the message. The only difference is that the original message will be included in the body of the e-mail.

# Organizing E-Mail

Once you get started e-mailing, it won't be long before your Inbox is full of messages. Sorting through all your mail may pose a challenge, but Linspire is up to the task. There are a variety of features included in the e-mail program that will allow you to sort, organize and find e-mail.

## Searching Messages

Finding messages is a breeze in Linspire. You simply type the keywords that you are looking for in the search box and all the messages that match that criteria will appear.

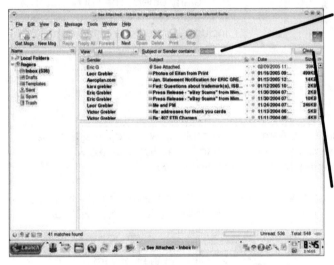

1. Type the keyword(s) in the field provided. The keyword can be the name of the person who sent you the message or any words in the subject line.

2. Press the Enter key. All messages that match the criteria you set will be displayed in the window as you type.

3. Click the Clear button to clear the search and return to see all the messages in your inbox.

## Sorting

Another way to quickly find a message is to use the sort functionality. Across the top of the message window you'll find different column headings. You can click on any of these headings to sort by that column. For example, if you wanted to put all of your messages in alphabetical order you could click on the Sender heading.

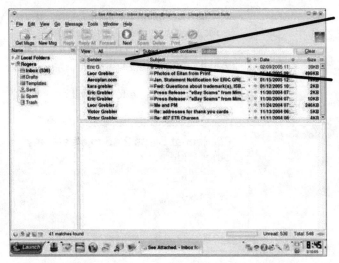

1. Click on the column that you would like to sort. The messages will be sorted in ascending order.

2. Click on the same column that you clicked on in Step 1 to sort the column in descending order. You can also tell which column has been selected because there will be a little green arrow in the column heading. An arrow pointing up means the column is sorted in ascending order and if it is pointing down, the column is sorted in descending order.

# Using Folders

All of the messages you receive are stored in a folder called the Inbox. Just as you can use folders on your computer to store your different files, so to can you use folders when dealing with e-mails. The types of folders you create are up to you, but typically people create folders to store messages from specific people or specific topics or projects. Once you have your folders created, you can add messages to them simply by clicking and dragging.

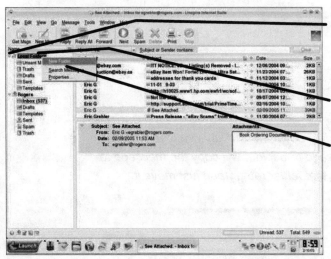

1. Click the triangle beside Local Folders to see a list of folders already created for you by the e-mail package.

2. Right-click on the word Local Folders. A menu will appear.

3. Click New Folder... The New folder dialog box will open where you can name your newly created folder.

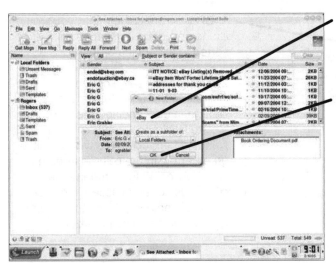

4. Type a name for your folder. It's a good idea to give it a name that describes the type of messages that you'll be including within.

5. Click OK. The folder will be created.

6. Repeat Steps 2 - 5 to create any other folders.

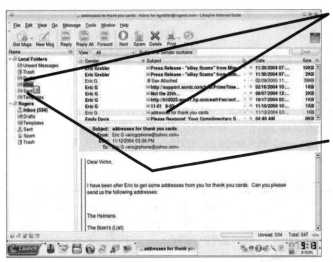

7. Click and drag any message from the window onto any of the folders that you created. When the message is over the folder, the folder name will be highlighted. When you release the mouse button, the message will be moved to that folder.

8. Click on any folder to reveal its contents.

*Holding down the Ctrl key when you drag a message to a folder will copy the message to that folder rather than just move it.*

# Trashing Messages

Removing an e-mail message is very similar to removing files on your computer. When a message is deleted, it is actually just sent to a folder called Trash. Once you empty messages out of the trash, they will be permanently deleted.

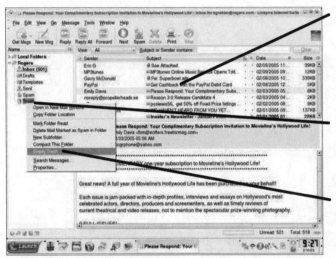

1. Click on a message you would like to delete. It will be highlighted.

2. Press the Delete key on your keyboard. The message will be sent to the Trash folder.

3. Right-click on the Trash Folder. A menu will appear. Make sure that it is the Trash folder under your ISP, not the one under Local Folders.

4. Click Empty Trash. All the folders in your Trash will be permanently deleted.

*When you are deleting a message, you can bypass the Trash by holding down the Shift key while you press the Delete key.*

# Instant Messaging

**13**

Think of instant messaging as e-mail on steroids. While e-mail has so many advantages over traditional mail, instant messaging takes things a few steps further. Instant messaging allows you to conduct online chat sessions so that you can rapidly communicate with another party. Unlike e-mail, you can always tell whether or not the person you are sending a message to is online, you don't have to wait several minutes for the message to arrive, and you don't have to periodically check an inbox. Once you create a list of people that you want to communicate with, you can always tell if those people are online and available for a chat session.

As its name would suggest, in instant messaging, when you type a message, the recipient receives that message instantly. Beyond just chatting back and forth with text, you can send files, add expressions to your messages, share web links, photos, music, and do much more.

In this chapter we'll cover:

- Setting up an Instant Messenger account

- Creating a contact list

- Sending and receiving messages

- Sharing files and other content

# Creating an Instant Messaging Account

There are a wide range of different instant messaging services that are supported in Linspire. Before you can begin instant messaging, you'll need to set up an account with one of these providers. Not all messaging services can communicate with one another, so I would recommend finding out what services your friends use; otherwise, go with AIM as it is the most popular. The following instructions will show you how to create an AIM account, but the process of creating an account with other providers is similar.

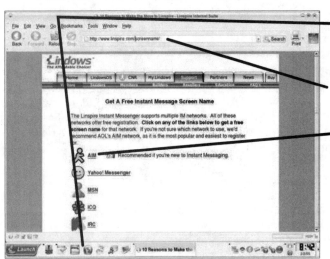

1. Click the Web Browser button in the Quick Launch bar. The Web Browser will open.

2. Type www.linspire.com/screenname in the Location bar.

3. Click on the AIM link. You'll be taken to a web page where you can create an account.

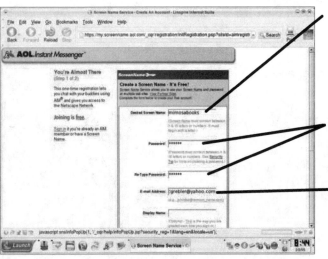

4. Type in a desired screen name. Keep in mind that there are millions of users of AIM so you'll have to create a fairly unique ID or it's a good likelihood someone else already has it.

5. Type and re-type your password in the fields provided. It will appear as a series of stars.

6. Type in your e-mail address in the field provided.

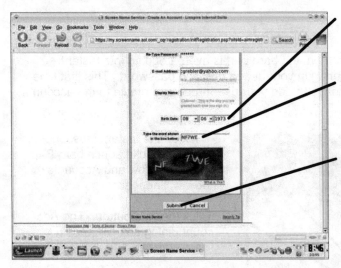

7. Click the drop-down arrows to enter the day, month, and year of your birth date.

8. Type in the word that you see in the graphic. This is a security feature that prevents computers from creating automatic accounts.

9. Click the Submit button.

*There's a good likelihood that the screen name you chose is taken as there are millions of AIM users. If a screen appears telling you your name is taken, simply enter a new one.*

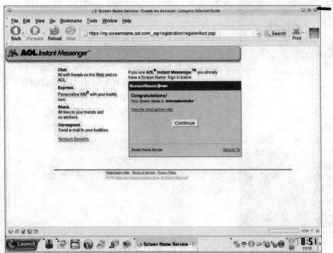

10. Close the web browser when the Congratulations screen appears. You are now ready to launch instant messenger.

# Logging Into Instant Messenger

Now that you have an account created, the hard part is over. Logging into Instant Messenger is just a matter of entering in your user name and password. This first time you launch the program, you will have to add your user name and profile to the accounts list.

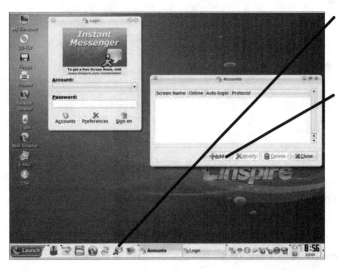

1. Click on the Instant Messenger icon in the Quick Launch bar. Both the Login window and Accounts window will appear.

2. Click the Add button. The Add Account dialog box will appear.

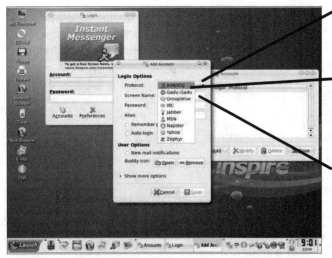

3. Click on the down arrow beside Protocol. A list of instant messenger providers will appear.

4. Click on the profile associated with your user name and password. For example, if you signed up for an AIM account, click the AIM/ICQ option.

5. Type in your screen name, password and alias in the fields provided.

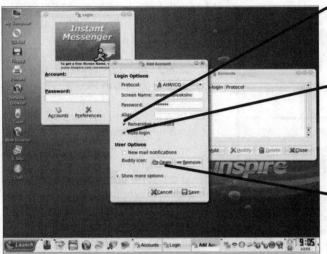

6. Click the check box beside Remember password. This way you won't be prompted for your password when you login.

7. Click the check box beside Auto-login if you don't want to be prompted to enter your account and password when you start Instant Messenger. Check this option if you only have one account.

8. Click the Open button. You can now choose a photo to use as your buddy icon. This is the image people will see in their messenger window when chatting with you.

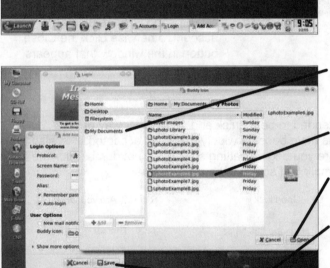

9. Navigate to the location that contains the image you would like to use as your buddy icon.

10. Click on the desired photo. It will be highlighted.

11. Click Open. The file will be selected as your buddy icon.

12. Click Save. The account will be added to the Accounts list.

13. Repeat Steps 2 - 12 to add any other accounts that you may have created.

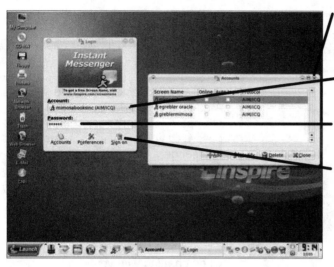

14. Click the Close button to close the accounts window when you are finished adding accounts.

15. Select your account from the Accounts drop-down list.

16. Type in your password if it does not already appear.

17. Click Sign on. You will now be signed on. The first time you sign on you will be prompted to sign up for a free SIPphone account. If this is something you're interested in, you can proceed with creating an account, otherwise click the Close button in the window that appears.

# Chatting Acronyms

Because instant messaging is intended to be a quick and convenient way of communicating, several acronyms have become widely used and accepted. It is wise to understand these acronyms before you begin chatting so you are not dumbstruck the first time you see them. Here is a sampling of some of the most popular:

| | | |
|---|---|---|
| LOL. Laugh out loud | GL. Good luck | RUOK? Are you OK? |
| BRB. Be right back | HTH. Hope this helps | THX. Thanks |
| CFN. Ciao for now | IMS. I am sorry | NP. No problem |
| FYI. For Your Information | ROTFL. Rolling on the floor laughing | YT? You there? |

*A long list of common acronyms that can be used in instant messaging can be found at www.aim.com.*

# Adding Buddies

Before you can begin chatting, you'll need someone to chat with. If you have friends already using instant messaging you can add their screen names to your buddy list.

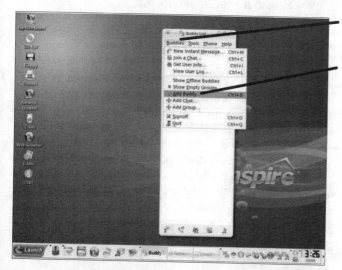

1. Click Buddies from the menu bar. A list of options will appear.

2. Click Add Buddy... The Add Buddy dialog box will appear.

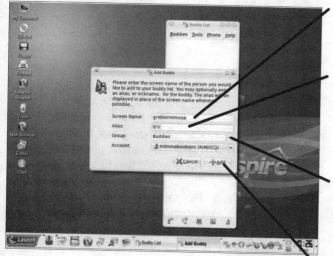

3. Type in the screen name of your buddy. This is the only field that you must enter; all others are optional.

4. Type a nickname or alias for this buddy if desired. It's a good idea to type a nickname if the screen name of the person you are adding is so obscure that you wouldn't know who it was just by looking at it.

5. Click the down arrow and select a group that you would like to add this buddy to. You'll be learning more about creating groups later in this chapter.

6. Click the Add button to add this buddy to your list.

# Grouping Buddies

If you are going to have more then a few buddies, it's a good idea to categorize them into groups. Rather than scrolling through a large list of buddies when you're looking for someone's screen name, you can simply look to a specific group.

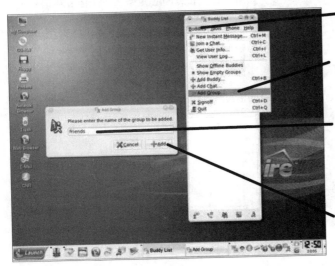

1. Click Buddies. The Buddies menu appears.

2. Click Add Group... A dialog box will appear where you can type a name for your group.

3. Type a name for the group. Typical group names are family, friends, or coworkers, but you can give the group any name you choose.

4. Click Add. The group now appears in your buddy list.

5. Repeat Steps 1 - 4 to add any other groups.

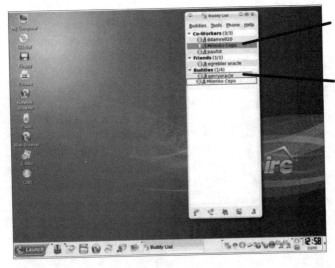

6. Position your mouse pointer over any buddy that you would like to move to a particular group.

7. Click and drag that buddy anywhere under the group heading that you would like to add them to.

8. Release the mouse button. They will be moved to that group.

# Chatting

This is the easiest part. Simple double-click on the name of any buddy that is currently online and you can begin your chatting session. There are a variety of tools you can use to change how your information is displayed during the chat session.

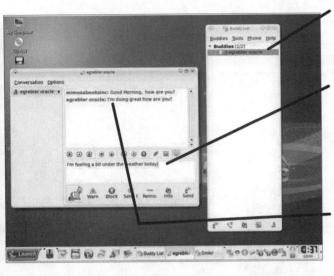

1. Double-click on any buddy on your list that is currently online. A window will appear where you can begin chatting.

2. Type your message in the bottom part of the window and press Enter. The text will appear in the top half of the window. Both you and the person you are chatting with will be able to see all the contents of the top half of the window.

3. View their reply. The screen name of the person you are chatting with will appear in red, while your name will appear in blue.

## Formatting Messages

When you speak with someone on the phone, you are able to show emotion by changing the volume of your voice or by adding inflections. You can use formatting to convey your feelings and emotions when instant messaging. You can even add little smiley icons to further convey your emotions.

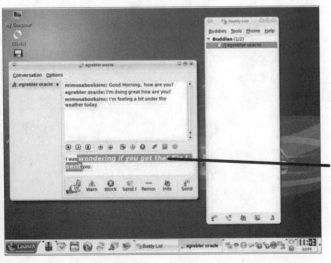

1. Click and drag across the message text that you would like to format. It will be highlighted. Alternatively, you can change formatting settings before you begin to type.

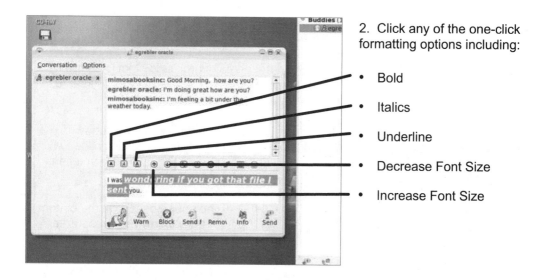

2. Click any of the one-click formatting options including:

- Bold

- Italics

- Underline

- Decrease Font Size

- Increase Font Size

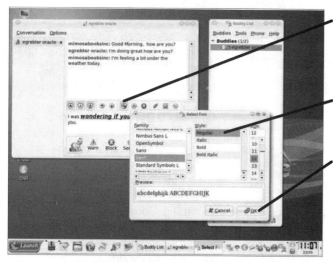

3. Click the Font Face button if you want to change the font of the selected text. A dialog box will appear.

4. Click on the desired font face, style and size. They will be highlighted when selected.

5. Click OK. The font will be applied to the selected text.

*Capitalizing all letters of a word is the equivalent of SHOUTING when instant messaging.*

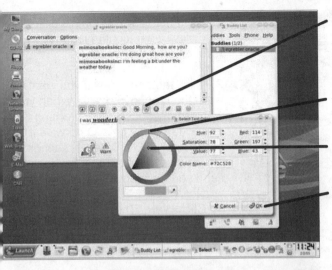

6.  Click on the Foreground font color button if you want to change the color of your font.  A dialog box will appear.

7.  Click anywhere on the circle to change the hue level.

8.  Click anywhere in the triangle to select a color.

9.  Click OK and the color will be applied.

10.  Repeat Steps 7 - 9 with the Background font color if so desired.

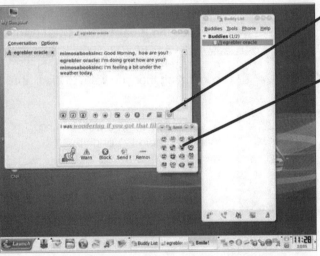

11.  Click on the Insert smiley button. A menu of different smiley emotion icons will appear.

12.  Click on the desired icon.  It will be added to your message.

## Warning and Blocking Users

There may be times when you are chatting with people unfamiliar to you and they may say something offensive.  You have the ability to warn users to let them know that their comments are unwelcome. The person you are warning doesn't have to know it's you sending the warning as they can be sent anonymously.  After repeated warnings, the user will no longer be able to send you messages.  You also have the ability to block any users from sending you messages at all.

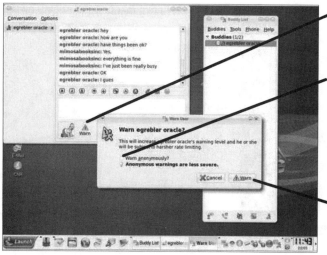

1. Click the Warn button. A dialog box will appear, confirming that you want to warn that user.

2. Click the check box if you want to warn them anonymously. When you warn anonymously, their warning level goes up by 5%. Otherwise it goes up by 20%. When it reaches 100%, they will no longer be able to send you messages.

3. Click Warn. The dialog box will close and you will be returned to your session.

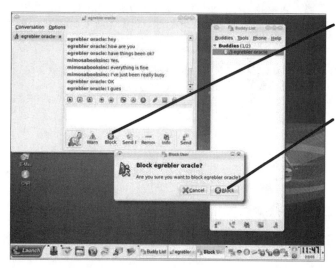

4. Click the Block button if you want to block a user from sending you messages. A dialog box will appear, confirming that you want to block that user.

5. Click Block. The user will no longer be able to send you messages.

## Sending Files

One of the major limitations of e-mail is that you are typically limited to the file size that you can send as an attachment. Not so with Instant Messenger. You can send files as large as you want directly to the person you are chatting with.

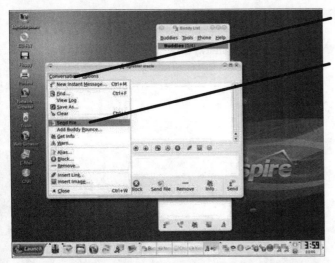

1.  Click Conversation. The Conversation menu appears.

2.  Click Send File... The Send File dialog box opens allowing you to select a file to transfer.

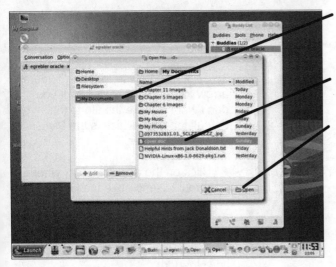

3.  Navigate to the folder that contains the file that you would like to send.

4.  Click on the desired file. It will be highlighted.

5.  Click Open. The file will sent to the recipient.

# Receiving Files

While most e-mail programs have filters that will disallow suspect files from being accepted, Instant Messenger has no such filter. With that being said, before you accept any files, make sure you know the person who is sending it to you to avoid accepting potential viruses.

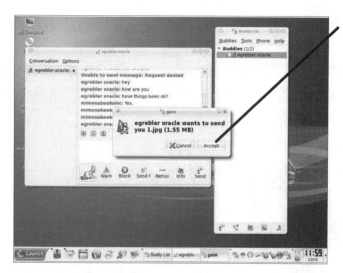

1. Click the Accept button to accept the file that is being sent. Another dialog box will appear where you can choose where to save the file.

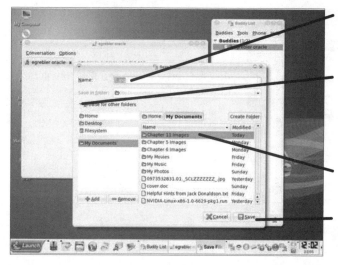

2. Type a new name for the file if you don't want to accept the default name.

3. Click the Browse for other folders arrow to expand the window if you don't want to save the file to the default location, which is the My Documents folder.

4. Click on the desired folder where you would like to save the file.

5. Click Save. The File Transfers dialog box will appear. It will close automatically when the file has been downloaded.

*Beside the group headings in your buddy list there are two numbers in brackets, e.g. (2/3). In this example, it means 2 out of the 3 contacts in this group are available for chatting.*

# Away Message

There's nothing worse the sending someone an instant message and not getting a response because that person in away from their computer. If you are logged on to Instant Messenger but are unavailable for conversations, you should create an away message that notifies people that you are away from your computer. By default, if you are away from your computer for 15 minutes, the away message appears automatically.

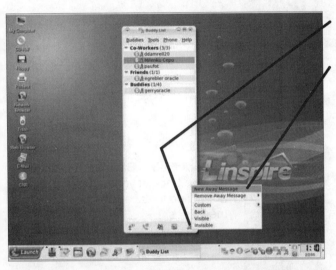

1. Click the Away Message button. A menu will appear.

2. Click New Away Message. A dialog box will open where you can create and save an away message.

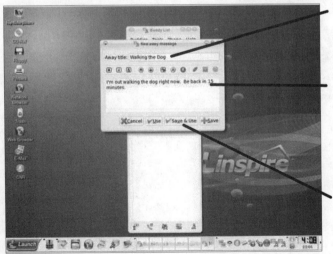

3. Type a name for your away message. This is how you will identify the message when selecting away messages.

4. Type the desired message to let the people who send you a message know that you are away. If you like, you can add details like where you are, how they can contact you or when you'll be back.

5. Click the Save & Use button if you want to use that away message right now. Alternatively just click the Save button to use the away message later.

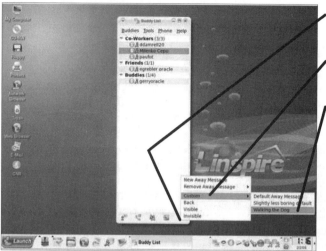

6. Click the Away Message button. A menu will appear.

7. Click Custom. A list of your saved away messages will appear.

8. Click the desired message.

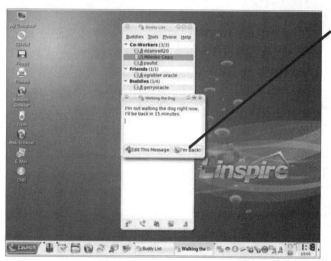

9. Click the I'm Back! button when you are back at your computer and are willing to accept instant messages.

# Home Networking

**14**

A friend of mine was over the other day and he was fascinated when I saved a digital photo I was working on at my upstairs computer directly to a computer in the basement. That's the beauty of networks - no matter what computer you are working on, you have access to all of the others on the network.

People, especially those new to the world of computing, get very nervous when they hear the word networking. Visions of high-speed cables, computer geeks, smoking computers, and hours of lost time and frustration might fill your head, but these are all misconceptions. If you're unfamiliar with the term networking or networks – in a nutshell, it's when two or more computers communicate with each other. If you have two or more computers in your home, you can create your own home network. The advantages of home networks are numerous and include sharing hardware devices like printers and scanners, sharing files, sharing a single Internet connection and playing games with multiple users. Your Linspire computer actually makes it a piece of cake to communicate with other computers on your home network, regardless of the operating system each computer is running.

In this chapter we'll cover:

- Connecting to other computers
- Sharing files and folders
- Transferring files

# Setting Up a Home Network

Setting up a home network isn't as hard as it may seem, and the benefits far outweigh the investment it takes to get your network up and running. There are entire books dedicated to the subject, but here we will just cover the basics.

As far as hardware is concerned there are only a few things that you need. First and foremost is more than one computer, and all of the computers must have an Ethernet connection. Although it is possible to set up a home network through a dial-up modem, that goes beyond the scope of this book. The computers should also all be connected through a router, either by cable or a wireless connection.

Once the hardware is set up you must configure your network. How a network is configured depends on the operating system of each of the computers on the network. Linspire itself will automatically recognize all other computers on a network.

# The Network Share Manager

The Network Share Manager is really your one-stop shop for setting up and viewing computers on your network. Within the Network Share Manger you can look for computers, view their shared folders and set up a network.

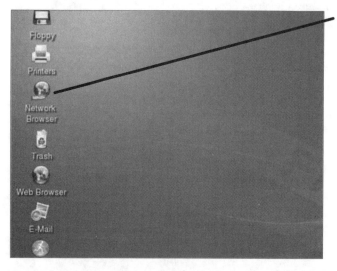

1. Double-click the Network Browser icon on your desktop. The Network Share Manager will open.

# Finding Computers on Your Network

Linspire will automatically recognize all of the computers that are attached to your network.

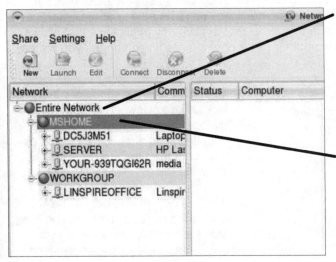

1.  Double-click on Entire Network. All of the workgroups on your network will appear. A workgroup is simply a category name that you give to a group of computers, files or folders that belong to a network. Later you'll learn to create and name a workgroup.

2.  Double-click on a workgroup. All of the computers on the network that fall under that workgroup will appear.

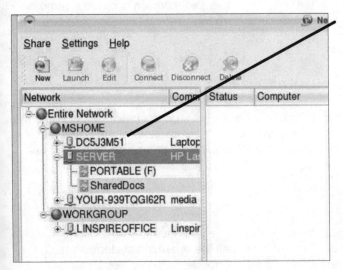

3.  Double-click on a computer. All of the folders on that computer that are shared and available to network users will appear.

# Mounting a Share

In order for you to view the contents of a folder on your network, the folder must first be mounted. Mounting basically means to install that folder so that it is viewable from your computer. Once a folder is mounted, you can view its contents as if the folder was actually on your computer, rather than on the network. You'll be able to access this shared program from the File Manager, your desktop or from any application that allows you to open files. You only have to mount a share once. Once it is mounted, you will always have access to it.

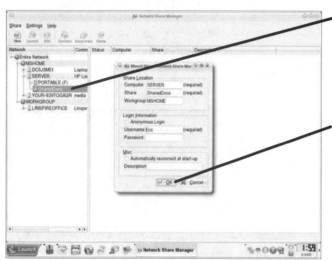

1. Double-click on the folder that you would like to view. The mount share dialog box will appear. All of the details should already be filled in as your computer recognizes it on the network.

2. Click OK. The folder will be added to your computer and the File Manager will launch, showing you the contents of that folder. An icon has also been added to your desktop so that you can always get back to this folder, which is called a remote share.

# Mounting Your Linspire Computer

Not only can you view files and folders from other computers on the network, but you can also make the files and folders on your Linspire computer available to other machines connected to the network. Before you can share folders, however, you will first need to mount your computer onto the network.

## Finding Your Computer Name

In order to mount your computer you will need the name you gave to your Linspire computer when it was first installed. If you didn't install the operating system yourself, the computer name can be found in the Control Center by following these steps.

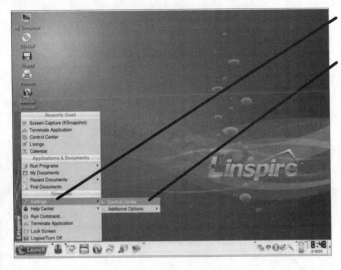

1. Click Launch | Settings.  A submenu will appear.

2. Click Control Center.  The Control Center will launch.

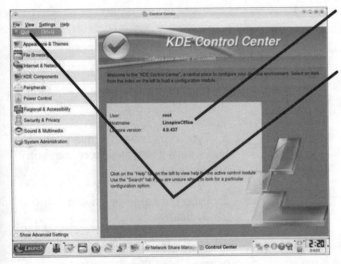

3. Take note of both the User and Hostname.  You will need both of these to mount your computer.

4. Click File | Quit to close this window and return to the Network Share Manager.

## Setting a Network Password

The network you set up needs to be secure to avoid unwanted, uninvited visitors. Imagine the damage that could be done if someone had full access to your computer. For this reason, a password for networking needs to be set up before you can mount your computer.

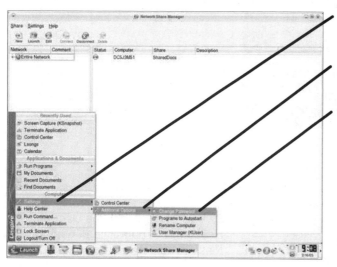

1. Click Launch | Settings. A submenu will appear.

2. Click Additional Options. Another submenu will appear.

3. Click Change Password. The Change password dialog box will appear.

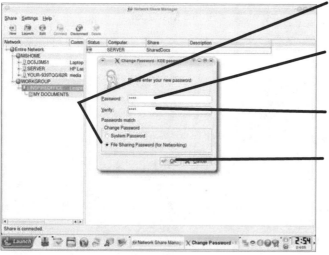

4. Click the radio button beside File Sharing Password.

5. Type a password for file sharing. Make sure it is a password that you'll remember.

6. Type the same password in the Verify field.

7. Click OK. The dialog box will close. Click OK again when a confirmation dialog box appears.

# Creating a Mount for Your Computer

Now that you know your computer's name and your User ID and password, you have all the information necessary to share your computer on the network.

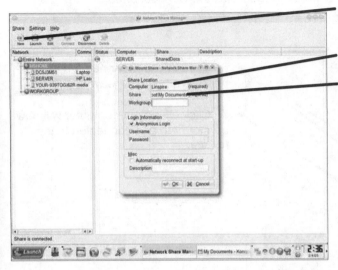

1. Click the New button. The Mount Share dialog box will open.

2. Type the name of your computer.

3. Type in a share. A share is a folder on your computer that you would like to share on the network. You'll be learning how to share other folders later in this chapter, but to start, you must share one folder when mounting your computer. Type \root if you want to grant access to your entire computer. Otherwise type \ and any folder. More on folders and their names can be found in the chapter entitled "File Management."

4. Type in the name of the workgroup you would like to add this computer to. If you'd like you can create a new workgroup for this computer simply by typing the name of a workgroup that doesn't already exist. Alternatively, you can leave this blank.

5. Click OK. Your computer can now be accessed by other computers on the network. Note that at this point only the folder that you specified in the share field can be viewed. Since you didn't enter your user name and password, you'll be prompted to do so before the computer can be mounted.

*When you restart your computer, your network shares will be disconnected. To reconnect to the shares, click the desired mount in the Network Share Manager then click the Connect button.*

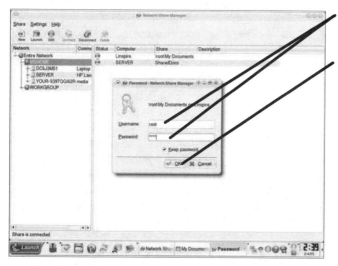

6.  Type in your user name and password for your network.

7.  Click OK. Your computer will now be mounted and connected to the network.

## Sharing Folders

When you mounted your computer, you selected one folder to be shared. You can make any folder on your computer accessible on the network by sharing it. There are a variety of ways in which a folder can be shared, but the easiest is through the File Manger.

1.  Click on the File Manager icon in the Quick Launch bar. The File Manger will launch.

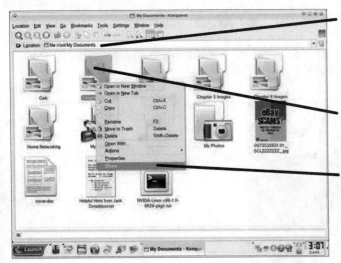

2.  Navigate to the folder that contains a folder that you would like to share.  More on navigating for files and folders can be found in the chapter entitled "File Management."

3.  Right-click on the folder that you would like to share.  A menu will appear.

4.  Click Share.  A dialog box will appear.

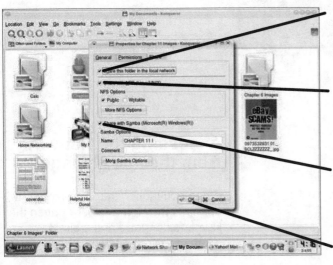

5.  Click the check box entitled Share this folder in the local network.  A variety of options will now become available.

6.  Click the check box if you want to give access to this folder to Linux-based or Unix-based computers on the network.

7.  Click the Share with Samba check box if you want to give access to this folder to Microsoft Windows-based computers on the network.

8.  Click OK.  The folder will now be accessible on the network.

# Accessing the Network

Once you have your folders shared and your network set up, you can actually access it from multiple locations, including your desktop, the File Manager, the Network Share Manager and program dialog boxes.

## Accessing the Network from Your Desktop

Whenever you create a mount to a shared folder on your network, an icon will appear on your desktop with a shortcut to that folder on the network.

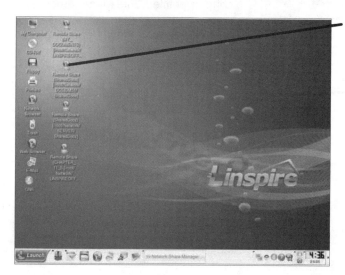

1. Double-click on the Remote Share icon on the desktop. The File Manger will open, revealing the contents of the shared folder on the network.

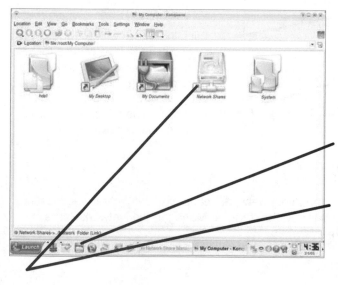

## Accessing the Network from the File Manager

When you launch the File Manger, it opens to the Home folder. Within the Home folder you'll find a direct shortcut to your network.

1. Click on the File Manager icon on the Quick Launch bar. The File Manger will open.

2. Click on the Network Shares shortcut. All of the shared folders on your network will now be displayed, regardless of what workgroup they belong to.

*Files and folders on your network can be moved, copied, pasted and opened like any other files on your computer. See the chapter "File Management" to review these features.*

## Accessing the Network from Dialog Boxes

Whenever you open or save a file in almost any program, a dialog box appears where you can navigate your computer to select the appropriate folder. When you have a network set up, you can access shared folders on the network directly from these dialog boxes. The beauty of that is, rather than having to run around the house with disks when you want to open or save a file from a different computer, you can access them directly from your network.

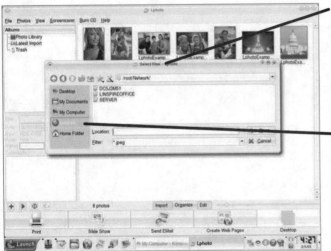

1. Access an Open or Save dialog box from within any program. In this example, we're using the Open dialog box from Lphoto. The dialog boxes in each program are slightly different, but most should give you access to your network.

2. Click on the Network option. A list of folders that are available on your network will appear. You can then select these folders like you would any other folder on your local hard drive.

*The dialog boxes in some programs do not provide you with a direct link to your network. When browsing, you can find all the computers in your network in the folder /root/Network.*

# Getting Help

**15**

Help? What do you need help for? You've got this book! Believe it or not this book doesn't have all the answers to Linspire. Truth be told, it would take a series of encyclopedias to cover all of the possible topics, configurations, and potential situations that may arise from using your Linspire computer. If you do get stuck along the way, don't worry as Linspire has a variety of ways to help you dust off and get back on your feet again.

The first thing that you need to determine is what type of learner you are. Do you prefer to sit back and relax as someone explains things to you, do you like to dig right in and help yourself, or do you prefer to read about a topic thoroughly to understand it? Regardless of the type of learner you are, Linspire has a solution for you.

In this chapter we'll cover:

- Asking Linspire support for help
- Navigating the FAQs
- Searching the knowledgebase

# Using the Knowledgebase

Although the technology in Linspire may seem new to you, understand that there are many people who forged a path before you, and you can benefit from their experience. Within Linspire there is a knowledgebase that is filled with answers to questions that have been previously asked.  If you're having a problem, there's a good likelihood that someone else has had this problem in the past and that the answer is in the knowledgebase.  You can quickly search the knowledgebase for a question that is similar to yours to see if an answer has been provided.  Typically, the knowledgebase is the first place you should go to for help.

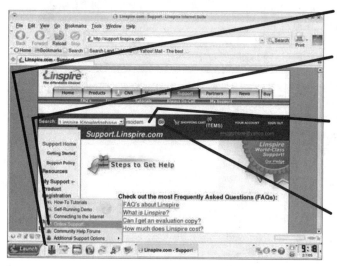

1.  Click the Help Center button.  A menu of help options will appear.

2.  Click Online Support.  The Web Browser will launch and will open to the Linspire support page.

3.  Type the keywords of your question in the field.  For example, if you were having a problem with your modem, you would type the word modem in the field.

4.  Click the Go button.  The knowledgebase will search for questions that have the word modem in them.

The Linspire Knowledgebase is a web-based support feature.  This means that you must be connected to the Internet in order to take advantage of this help feature.

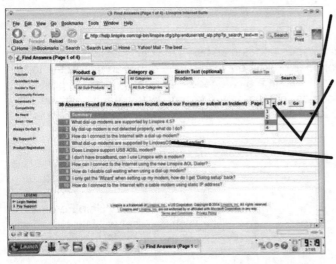

5. Scroll through the questions to see if there is one that is similar to the problem you are having.

6. Click on the page drop-down button if you want to proceed to another page of questions that contain your keyword.

7. Click on a question. The screen will change to provide you with the answer to that question.

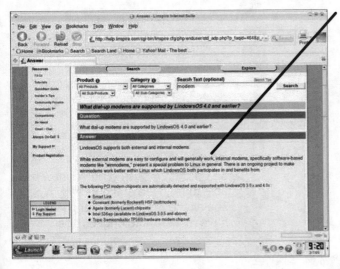

8. Review the answer. If it answers the question that you had you can close the browser by clicking the Close button in the top right corner. If your question was not answered, you can repeat Steps 3 - 6 to search the knowledgebase again, or you can proceed to one of the other help methods.

# Using Community Forums

People who use Linux-based operating systems are a tight knit group, and as a Linspire user, you'll be instantly welcomed into this community. The community help forum is a place where users can have discussions, share tips and tricks and also pose questions for other users to answer.

# Viewing the Forum

The best way to learn more about Linspire and find answers to your questions is to simply browse through the forum. The forum is broken down in a type of hierarchy. At the top you have various general categories. Within the categories, you have posts. A post is a comment or question that someone has "posted" to the forum. Within each post you will find a discussion string. The discussion string is a list of all the responses that people have made to the post.

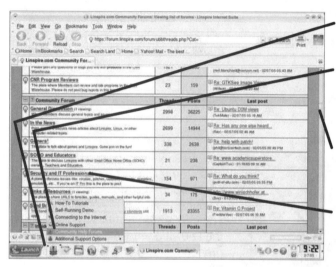

1. Click the Help Center button. A menu of help options will appear.

2. Click Community Help Forums. The Web Browser will launch and will open to the Linspire Community page.

3. Scroll through the different forum categories until you find one of particular interest to you.

4. Click on a category. A variety of posts that fall under that category will appear.

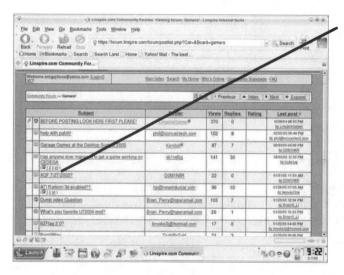

5. Click on a post. You will now be able to read the entire thread. You'll see all the responses that people have made to the original post.

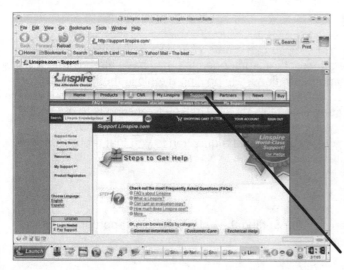

## Searching the Forum

If you've run across a problem that you couldn't find an answer for on the support page, the next best place to look is the forum. There's a good likelihood that if you are having a problem, others have also experienced this problem and that there is a discussion thread that covers the solution. Within the forum you have the ability to search for a specific topic rather than simply browsing.

1. Click on the Support tab. This will take you back to the main support page regardless of where you are in the forum.

2. Scroll down until you see a section called Step 3, Visit our community forums.

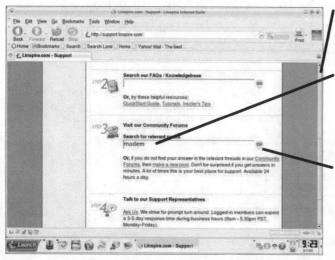

3. Type in a keyword for the subject you are trying to get help with. For example, if you are having trouble with your modem, type in the word modem.

4. Click Go. All of the posts that have the word modem in them will appear. You can then scroll through and click on any of the posts to view their entire threads. If you don't find the answers that you are looking for, you can either create your own post, as covered in the next section or you can contact Linspire support directly. Contacting support is covered later in this chapter.

## Creating and Replying to Posts

If you don't find an answer to your query, you can create your own post on the forum. As mentioned earlier, if you are having a problem, someone else may have already had the problem or may be sharing the same frustrations. By posting a topic in the forum you can sometimes get answers faster then you would from support, and you are helping out your fellow Linspire users by bringing attention to this topic. The key to posting is to put your message in the correct category. You can also reply to existing posts if you have something valuable to add or if someone has posed a question to you that requires a reply.

## Creating a Post

Creating a post is really quite simple. After finding the category that is appropriate for your post, you simply type your message.

*Before you can create a post in the forums, you must first be logged on. If you are unable to create a post, click the My.Linspire tab and log on using your CNR user name and password.*

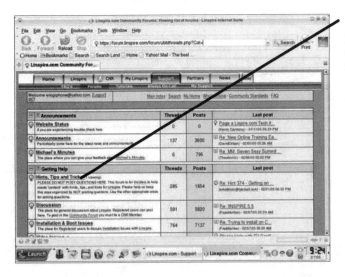

1. Click on the category under which you would like to create a post. A list of all the postings under that category will appear.

*In most forum areas there is a posting entitled "Read This Before Posting Here!" Click on this link before posting to read what posts, if any, are acceptable in that forum.*

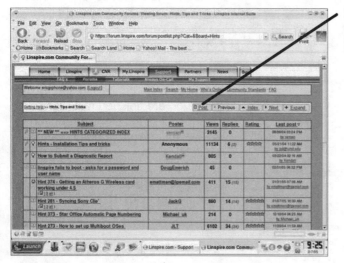

2. Click the Post button. The screen will change and you will now be able to enter the text for your post.

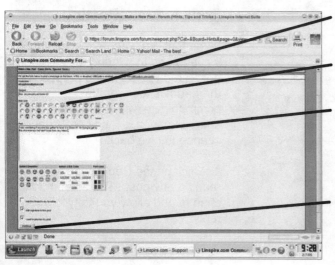

3. Type a subject for your posting. Try to be as specific as possible.

4. Click on the radio button beside an emotion icon if so desired.

5. Type your post and provide as much information as possible. The more information your provide, the greater the likelihood you'll get the answers you're looking for.

6. Click Continue. By default, you will be able to preview your message before it is posted. You can uncheck this option to instantly submit.

*Even though the Community Forum has its own navigation buttons, it's easiest to move back and forth through the forum using the Back and Forward buttons in the Web Browser.*

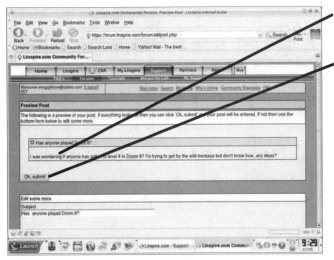

7. Review your message to ensure that it looks the way you want it to.

8. Click the Ok, submit button. Your message will be posted. Alternatively, you can scroll down and make any changes to your post. When you are finished making your changes, click the Continue button to preview the message again. After you submit, your post is now in the forum. You can return to the forum frequently to view the string and see who has responded.

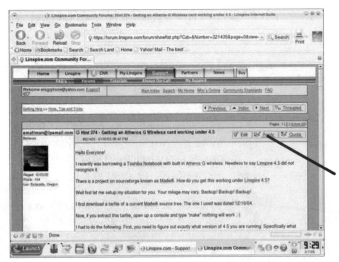

## Replying to a Posting

If you feel like you have something of value to add to a string, by all means, post a reply. The entire purpose of the forum is for users to communicate with each other, and to share experiences, so here's your chance to give back.

1. Click on the Reply button when reading any post. The screen will change and allow you to type your reply.

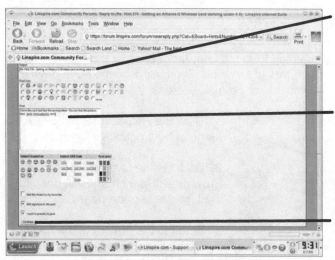

2.  Type a subject for your reply if you don't want to use the default subject that appears.  Typically, people leave the default subject as is.

3.  Type your reply in the area provided.  You can also apply formatting to your reply by clicking on a font color or clicking the radio button beside an emotion icon to be included in your message.

4.  Click the Continue button.  You will be able to preview your reply.

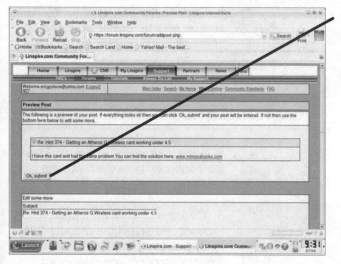

5.  Click the Ok, submit button.  Your reply will be posted.  Alternatively, you can scroll down and make any changes to your reply.  When you are finished making your changes, click the Continue button to preview the reply again.  After you submit, your reply will appear as part of the thread in the forum.

*The Community Forum isn't just for posting issues.  You can share experiences you've had, express opinions and discuss many topics.  Just make sure you are posting to the correct category.*

# Technical Support from Linspire

If you can't find the answer to your question from the knowledgebase or the forums you can submit the question directly to the gurus at Linspire. Typically it will take 3-5 days to get a response, which will be sent directly to your e-mail address.

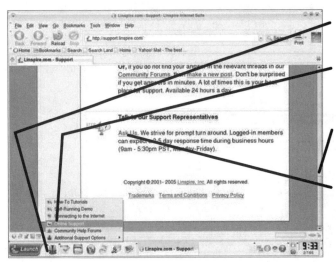

1. Click the Help Center button. A menu of help options will appear.

2. Click Online Support. The Web Browser will launch and will open to the Linspire support page.

3. Scroll to the bottom of the page where you'll see Step 4, Talk to our Support Representatives.

4. Click on the Ask Us link. You will now be able to provide your contact information and submit your question.

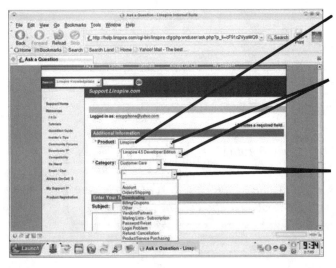

5. Type your e-mail address. This is the address where the response will be sent.

6. Click the drop-down menu beside Product and select the product that applies to you. Repeat the same for the subcategory drop-down menu that appears.

7. Click the drop-down menu beside Category and select the category that applies to you. Repeat the same for the subcategory drop-down menu that appears.

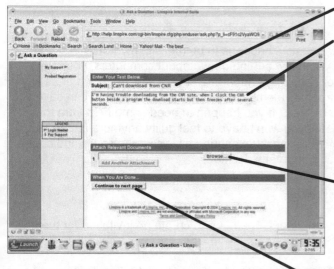

8.  Type a subject for your question.

9.  Type your question.  Be very specific about the issue you are having.  Also include any steps that you may have already taken to try and solve the problem.  The more information you provide the greater the likelihood that you'll get an answer that solves your problem.

10.  Click the Browse button if you have any files or documents related to the problem you are having that you would like to share.  A dialog box will appear where you can navigate for the file.

11.  Click the Continue to the next page button.

12.  Review the potential answers to your question.  If any address the topic you are looking for, you can click the link and read the answer. Otherwise proceed to Step 13.

13.  Click the Finish button.  Your question will be sent to Linspire. Check your e-mail account frequently as they've been known to beat expectations on the time it takes to get back to you.  A page will now appear with a reference number. Take note of that reference number as you can use it when communicating with Linspire.

# Sharing Desktops

Almost every family has a computer geek, it happens to be me with my family and you may be the one for your family. If you know a thing or two about computers, you may become the help desk guru for every uncle, grandparent, cousin and in-law who has a computer problem. I can't get your family members to stop calling you, but I can save you some time. The flip side may also be true. If you happen to need some help from that good-for-nothing-else relative, at least you won't have to feel guilty anymore because you now have the option of desktop sharing. Desktop sharing allows you to share and control other people's computers from your computer's desktop.

## Giving Control of Your Desktop

If you want to share your desktop with others, you need to create an invitation for them that includes the details of how they can connect.

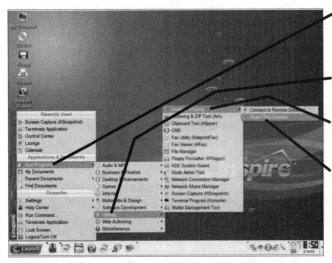

1. Click Launch | Run Programs. Categories of different programs will appear.

2. Click Utilities. A submenu of different utilities will appear.

3. Click Desktop Sharing. Another submenu will appear.

4. Click Share This Desktop. The Desktop Sharing program will launch.

*To share your desktop with others, you create an invitation that contains a host and password. That password and host will be valid for one hour from the time the invitation is created.*

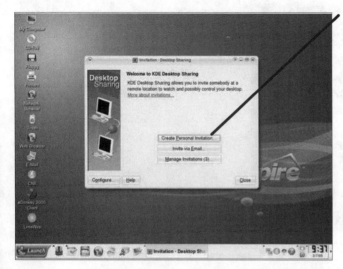

5. Click the Create Personal Invitation... button. A screen will appear providing you with a host and password that you can share with others who would like to connect to your desktop. Alternatively, you can click the Invite Via Email... button where you can compose an e-mail to the person or people with whom you would like to share your desktop.

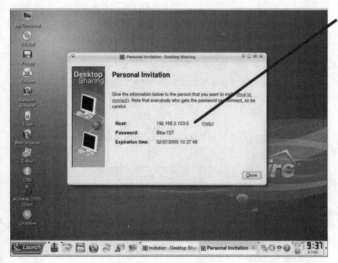

6. Take note of the host and the password. You can now pass this information on to the person with whom you would like to share your desktop. They will need a program that is called a VNC client in order to connect to and view your desktop. Proceed to the next section to learn about the VNC client on your Linspire computer. Once the person runs their VNC client to connect to your machine, a dialog box will appear asking you how you would like to handle the request to share your desktop.

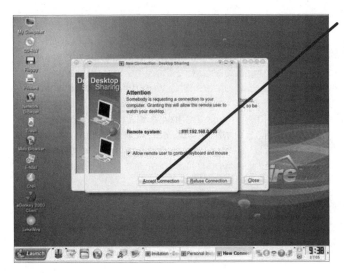

7. Click Accept Connection. Your invitee will now have complete access to your desktop.

*When the person you are sharing you desktop with closes their VNC client, you will get a message in your system tray notifying you that your desktop is no longer being shared.*

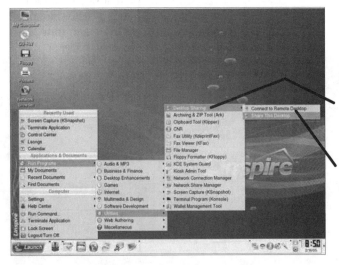

## Viewing Desktops

Not only can you share your desktop in Linspire, but you can also view the desktops of others.

1. Click Launch | Run Programs | Utilities. A list of utility programs will appear.

2. Click Desktop Sharing | Connect to Remote Desktop. A dialog box will appear where you can enter the host number.

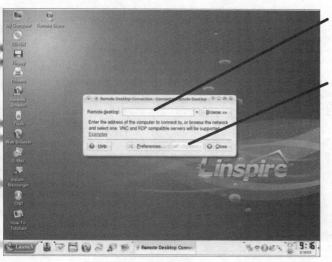

3.  Type in the host number that you were provided from the person who is sharing their desktop.

4.  Click Connect.  A dialog box will appear where you can select your type of Internet connection.

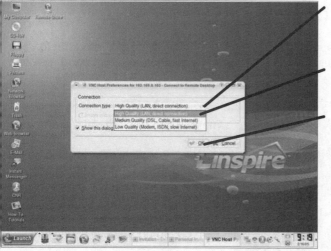

5.  Click the drop-down arrow to see a list of different types of Internet connections.

6.  Click the option that matches your type of connection.

7.  Click OK.  The person on the other end sharing their desktop will get a notification saying that you are trying to access their desktop.  As soon as they accept, a window will appear where you will need to type the password they provided you.

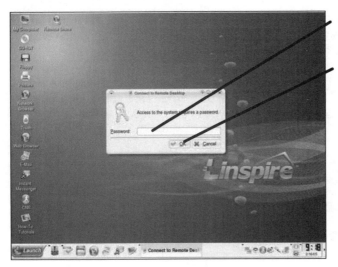

9. Type your password in the field provided.

10. Click OK. You will now have access to the shared desktop.

# Getting Program-Specific Help

If you are having issues within a specific application, you can look to that program for help. The help files differ drastically from one program to another, but in general, you can find help from the menu bar.

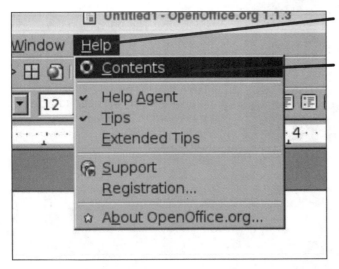

1. Click Help. Typically the Help menu is the last item on a menu bar.

2. Click Contents. Depending on the program you are working with, what happens next will differ. In most cases a window will be displayed where you can search for help based on a specific keyword.

# Printers

No operating system is an island, and Linspire is no exception. Typically you have several devices that work alongside your computer to make sure that it is a complete solution to your needs. The most common of these devices is a printer.

Let's face it, as convenient as computers are, most of us prefer to read documents from a piece of paper rather than a monitor. To do this, you need a printer installed and configured for your system. Linspire makes it easy for you to set up printers and other types of hardware that you'll use along side your computer.

In this chapter we'll cover:

• Setting up a printer

• Printing documents

**16**

# Adding a Local Printer

Despite of what you've heard, a local printer in not one that was born and lives in your city. That was poor attempt at a joke, I apologize. A local printer is actually one that is connected directly to your computer. Turn on your printer and make sure it is connected to your computer before you begin.

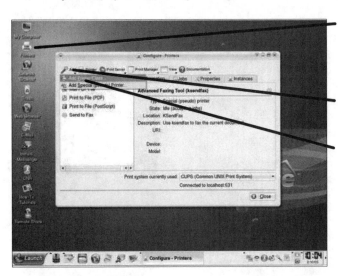

1. Double-click the Printers icon on the desktop. This will open the Printers window where you can add a printer.

2. Click the Add button. A menu will appear.

3. Click Add printer/class... The Add Printer wizard will appear and step you through the installation process.

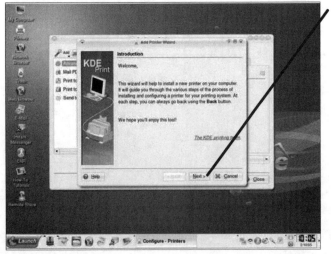

4. Click on Next. This will take you to the next step in the wizard.

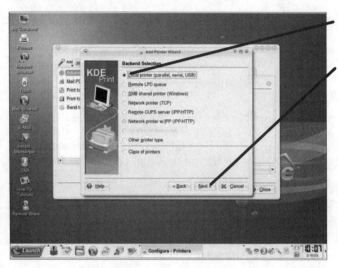

5. Click on the radio button beside the Local printer option.

6. Click on Next. The computer will now scan all of the ports to look for a printer connected to your machine.

*If you have a home network configured, you can select one of the network options to connect to a shared network printer.*

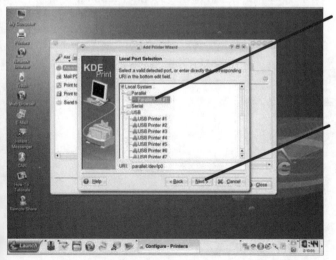

7. Click on the desired port selection. The port selection will depend on the type of printer connection you have. It can be Parallel, USB or if it's an older printer it may be Serial.

8. Click on Next. You'll proceed to the Printer model selection screen, where you'll be able to choose the model of your printer.

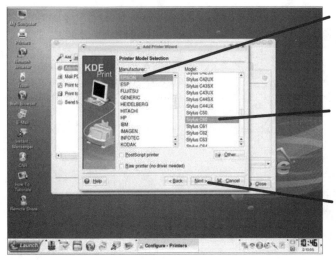

9.  Click on the manufacturer of your printer in the Manufacturer area of the window. A list of models that they make will appear in the Model area of the window.

10.  Click on the model of your printer. If you can't find your model, click on Other and select a model from the disk that came with the printer.

11.  Click on Next. You'll proceed to the Driver selection screen, where you can select the driver for your printer.

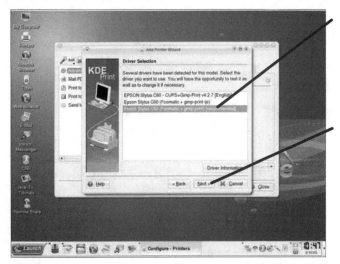

12.  Click on the appropriate driver. Typically one of the drivers will say recommended. If that is the case with the printer you selected, choose that option. If it's the wrong driver, you can change it after testing.

13.  Click Next. You will proceed to the next screen of the wizard, where you can test your printer.

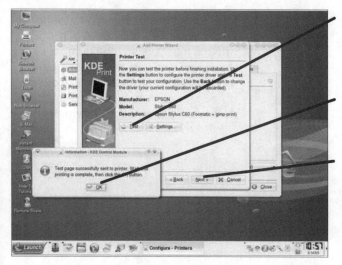

14. Click on Test. This will print a test page to confirm that your printer is working properly with the computer.

15. Click OK to close the dialog box that appears after the test page has been sent to the printer.

16. Click Next if the test page printed out normally. You'll proceed to the Banner selection screen. Alternatively, click on the Back button if the test print did not print out normally, then select a different driver.

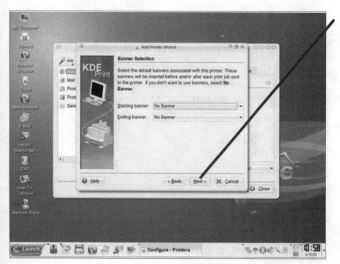

17. Click Next. Typically you don't need to print banners, which are a printed sheet before, or after, your print job describing what was printed. You will proceed to the Printer quota settings screen.

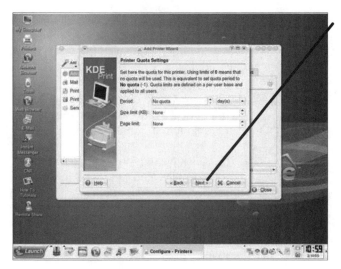

18.  Click Next, unless you want to set a quota for your printer. This means that you limit the number of pages printed in a certain time period and the size of files that are allowed to be printed. You will proceed to the Users access settings screen.

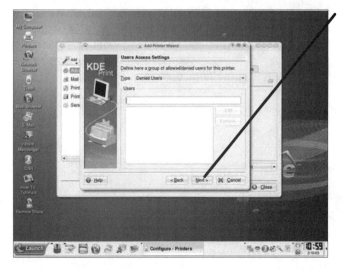

19.  Click Next, unless you want to limit who can use the printer. If so, you can set this in this screen. You will proceed to the General information screen.

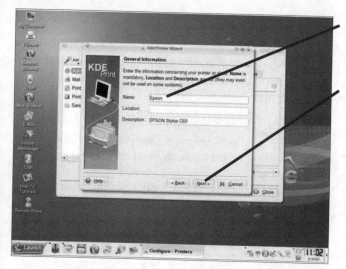

20. Type a name for the printer in the Name text box. The name cannot have any spaces in it.

21. Click Next, and you'll be taken to the Confirmation screen.

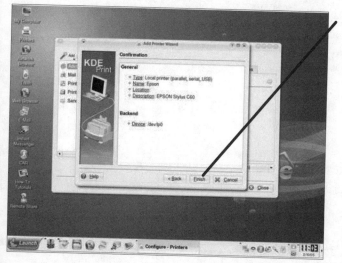

22. Click Finish after you've reviewed the settings. Your printer will now be set up and ready for printing.

# Printing

Printing works the same in almost every application that supports printing. If you have more than one printer connected to your machine, you'll simply pick the printer that you want to print to, select any additional options, and away you print!

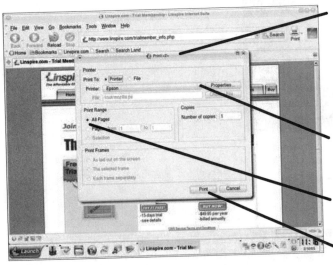

1. Execute the Print dialog box from any program that you would like to print from. In most cases you can bing this up by pressing Ctrl+P or clicking File | Print. In this example we'll be printing from the Web Browser.

2. Click on the drop-down list and select a printer to which you would like to send this file.

3. Adjust any of the options presented to you in the dialog box.

4. Click Print. Your file will be printed.

# Index